GEORG

THE FRIENDS,

AND

THE EARLY BAPTISTS.

BY

WILLIAM TALLACK,

Author of " Malta under the Phœnicians, Knights, and English,"
" Friendly Sketches in America," &c.

LONDON:

S. W. PARTRIDGE & CO., 9, PATERNOSTER ROW.

1868.

GEORGE FOX.

PREFACE.

THIS work is, it is believed, the first which has definitely and minutely traced the doctrines and constitution of Quakerism mainly to the early Baptists.

The review of the remarkable influence of Fox and the Friends in the various departments of Philanthropy, Social Progress, Political Reform, Literature, Science, and Commercial Enterprise, has also been carried farther into detail than in any other book hitherto issued.

A large number of works and papers have been consulted in the preparation of this Memoir, and have been freely quoted from, with the view of collecting together, in small compass, from widely-scattered sources, a comprehensive and interesting description of the life and influence of George Fox. Some particulars respecting him are here for the first time published. His private and personal characteristics, and the social and general aspect of his times, have received special attention.

The author has gratefully to acknowledge his obligations to his friends, William Beck of London, Charles Fox of Falmouth, and John Thompson of Hitchin, for their valuable aid. To the assistance of the former he has been chiefly indebted for collecting the proofs of the Baptist origin of the chief portion of the constitution of Quakerism.

CONTENTS.

CHAPTER III.

THE BAPTIST ORIGIN OF QUAKERISM IN GENERAL.

CHAPTER IV.

FOX'S FIRST MINISTRY IN THE MIDLANDS AND IN YORKSHIRE.

CHAPTER VII.

FOX'S FOREIGN MISSION JOURNEYS.

CHAPTER VIII.

PRIVATE LIFE AND PERSONAL CHARACTERISTICS OF FOX.

CHAPTER IX.

FOX'S ADDITIONS TO THE BAPTIST SYSTEM — THE QUAKER POLITY.

CHAPTER X.

LAST DAYS AND DECEASE.

GEORGE FOX,

THE FRIENDS, AND THE EARLY BAPTISTS.

CHAPTER I.

QUAKERISM, ITS CHARACTERISTICS AND REMARKABLE INFLUENCE UPON THE WORLD.

INFLUENCE OF GEORGE FOX THROUGH THE SOCIETY OR-
GANISED BY HIM—QUAKERISM AND RELIGIOUS FREEDOM—
THOROUGH CARE FOR THE POOR AS A CHURCH DUTY—
EDUCATION OF EVERY CHILD IN THE SOCIETY—ZEAL IN
SABBATH SCHOOL EFFORTS—QUAKER MISSIONS AT HOME
AND ABROAD—QUAKER LEADERSHIP IN THE GREAT PHI-
LANTHROPIC MOVEMENTS—FRIENDS AND POLITICS—SCIENCE
AND LITERATURE—QUAKERS' PROMINENCE IN BANKING,
MANUFACTURES AND TRADE—GREAT INFLUENCE OF QUAKER-
ISM IN THE UNITED STATES—EX-FRIENDS.

THE influence of the career of George Fox is best
appreciated by considering the subsequent character and
action of the Society of Friends, of which he was the
organiser. For few religious sects have been more
thoroughly moulded by their early leaders, and, so to

speak, stereotyped as to their future constitution, than
that Christian body. Let us then take a preliminary
glance at the prominent features of the Society, in order
the better to understand the importance of the life and
character of the subject of this work.

As respects their theological belief, the Friends have
never acknowledged any strictly defined creed, but have,
nevertheless, been generally successful in steering a middle
course between latitudinarianism on the one hand, and, on
the other, any such rigidity of doctrine as may be inconsistent with the exercise, by every individual member,
of a healthy free thought, recognising the Divine authority
of the Bible; but at the same time repudiating human
claims to prescribe authoritatively for others the meaning
and extent of scriptural doctrine.

Whilst eminently loyal to the civil government and
earthly monarch, they do not, in the slightest degree,
recognise the Sovereign's claim to be entitled "the Head
of the Church;" for they hold, practically as well as
theoretically, that the Lord Jesus Christ is the only real
possessor of that title. Similarly, any proclamations, from
Royalty or the Privy Council, ordering national manifestations of prayer, penitence, or thanksgiving, are, so far
as the Friends are concerned, respectfully ignored. The
King or Queen, the Archbishops or Bishops, are, in their
eyes, invested with no more religious authority, or ecclesiastical reverence, than the humblest Christians in the
land.

The Friend cherishes a special sense of his individual
and inalienable responsibility to God, before whose judgment seat he knows that each one must render a separate

untransferable account of the actions and omissions of
this life. Doubtless, many Christians, in various degrees,
entertain a sense of this, but the Friends carry the principle
further into their practice than most others. Even in
their own religious assemblies they do not enforce on
themselves detailed uniformity of system or action.
Probably in no other sect in Christendom are there
entertained so many shades of opinion on religious matters
as amongst the Friends; yet nowhere is there greater
harmony and brotherly love, or more practical respect
for the claims of moral and philanthropic duty as an
accompaniment of religious profession.

Whilst thus largely untrammelled by bonds of hierarchy
or rigid dogma, the Society of Friends unites in general
with the main body of the Church of Christendom (one
amid many diversities and temporary sects, actuated
widely by the same Divine Spirit, honouring and loving
the same Lord) in recognising the unity, yet triune
manifestation, of the Godhead, also the deity, expiatory
atonement, resurrection and ascension of the Lord Jesus
Christ, the ever-living King of his people. Their views
of the perceptible presence and guidance of the Holy
Spirit in the hearts of the obedient, are perhaps more
definite than those of any other denomination. They
repudiate (as a body, and on scriptural grounds,) the
lawfulness of war, state-churches, slavery, oaths, and
capital punishment. They also differ in some other
respects from most of their fellow Christians, as for instance in the non-payment of preachers, the absence of
collegiate or special training for ministerial service, the
permission of public religious instruction by women, and

B 2

the restriction of the nature of sacraments to a spiritual and invisible union with the Lord.

In connection with these views there are three very important characteristics of the Friends which claim special attention, viz. their freedom from the prevalent "one man system" in Church matters; their practical adoption of the great and praiseworthy principle, that it is a primary duty of every religious community to care for, and when necessary to maintain, its poorer members; and that it is a third requirement of the Church to secure to all the children of its adherents a good education to qualify them for religious, moral, and civil usefulness.

The Friends have carried out these three grand principles, unitedly, further than any other denomination has done, although the Moravians, the Methodists, the Jews, and some other bodies, share in a portion of these distinctions.

Firstly, as to the Friends' freedom from "the one man system" of most other denominations; they have thereby derived a special vigour and healthiness both of corporate and individual action. For recognising the scriptural truths, that "the manifestation of the Spirit is given to *every* man to profit withal," and that "the body is not one member but many," and knowing by long experience and observation, that qualifications for Christian service of a more or less religious nature are widely scattered amongst the members of every intelligent earnest-hearted community, the Friends in their Church arrangements *afford opportunities for the exercise* of these gifts. Hence their public devotions are not limited to listening to the ministry of one or more appointed individuals, but any member is at liberty to engage in prayer or exhortation, provided he believes it his duty to do so, on the occasion. Hence also, in the miscellaneous services of the Church, there is a wide distribution of functions and offices. Whether he avails himself of it or not, every Friend has a more or less open door for the exercise of the duties of ministry or of useful activity, which he may feel himself called to undertake in aiding and sharing in the Church action.

Lastly, as a consequence, it is observable that the Friends generally are characterised by a special aptitude for works of philanthropy, religious instruction, charitable administration, and for the business of committees of various kinds. Just as a vigorous course of muscular training develops every limb of the body, so does the Quaker system (when fairly carried out) develop the spiritual and executive energies of all its members.

The same principle of the distribution of Church service is carried out in numerous other matters, and especially in the general management of the Society, in the distribution of its funds, the care of its poor, and the arrangement of its varied efforts for the general and particular welfare of its own members or others. It is not to be denied that sometimes the Quaker officials manifest a disposition to attempt a degree of oligarchical and exclusive action, but the constitution of their body (as handed down by George Fox) is so unfavourable to the development of such exclusiveness, that it cannot make great or permanent advances where attempted. The Quaker founders laid the principles of their religious republic too strongly on the simple basis of Christian

brotherhood, to be removed without overturning the whole
constitution of the Society. And there are, in general,
vigilant eyes and active spirits on the watch to check and
repress religious or disciplinary assumptions in this peculiarly democratic yet remarkably harmonious community.

A Quaker " Yearly Meeting," or large administrative
gathering of the Society, is a sight worth beholding, for
the rare spectacle which it presents, of cordial harmony
and peace, combined with great freedom of speech, and
withal with much seriousness. In these and other
Quaker assemblies, questions are not settled by mere ma-
jorities. If there is such a difference of opinion that
present harmonious agreement is unattainable, the matter
is postponed or compromised. No cheers or sign of
applause are permitted. No votes of thanks are given;
there is little, if any, of that sickening mutual laudation
which so characterises the speakers at some religious
gatherings. One often hears of vigorous hisses being
raised at " Church Congresses," when some plain-spoken
clerical or lay member has ventured to express, however
respectfully and legitimately, sentiments differing from
those of the majority. But such unseemly manifestations
do not occur at Quaker congresses. Very recently at a
meeting (composed mainly of Ritualistic clergymen) at
St. James's Hall, the name of the pious and beneficent
Earl Shaftesbury was received with loud hisses by an
audience who welcomed with " thunders of applause " the
statements of Archdeacon Denison, that the gifts of the
Holy Spirit were solely conveyed by the outward visible
channels of Baptismal regeneration, and the Real Presence in the Communion Bread, and as administered only

by "the spirituality" (that is clergymen episcopally ordained). But in the Friends' assemblies such unseemly hisses and tumultuous noises would be attributed to spirits of far other than celestial source, nor would respectful dissentients be overwhelmed with shouts of "turn him out, turn him out," as raised on the above occasion.

As to the second great practical feature of the Friends' Society—their care of their own poor as a systematic duty of the Church as such—it is well known that members of this community are never chargeable to the poor's-rates, or appear as applicants for admission to "Union houses," although the Friends pay the same proportionate contributions to the general poor-rates as the members of other denominations. (The Jews also are highly exemplary in this respect.)

But the Society of Friends has outstripped all other Christian bodies in its systematic and comprehensive care for its own poor, whilst at the same time it has liberally and abundantly extended its beneficent care to the poor of other denominations in addition. The Friends' charity, although beginning at home, has not ended there.

Every poor Friend who may be unable to earn a livelihood usually receives aid from his brother members, to the extent of from £20 to £40 per annum (administered privately in general), according to age and infirmity. And this does not include the money spent upon the education of his offspring.

When the poorer Friends are out of a situation, they are often facilitated in obtaining employment by various arrangements, such as free registries, and by the aid of private inquiries for vacancies.

A large number of charitable bequests and special funds
has been appropriated for the local or general benefit of
the members of this religious community; so much so,
that in some districts there has been a danger at times of
the spirit of self-exertion not being sufficiently developed
on the part of the recipients of these very liberal
subsidies.

In addition to this testamentary and systematic care
for the poorer Friends, a large amount of private aid is
continually being extended to them.

If other denominations had bestowed upon their poor
a small proportion of the systematic and individualising
care exercised by the Friends in such cases, there would
not be the outrageous scandals upon English humanity
and civilisation which are continually cropping up in the
newspapers in connection with shamefully neglected poor-
houses and casual wards, to say nothing of the frequent
instances of starvation which the history of every winter
brings to light, as samples of a much larger number
which never attract any public attention at all. The best
administered poor-laws are a sorry substitute for the
exercise of individual Christian charity administered with
less publicity, and on the main basis of religious duty.

Charity enforced by law is *not* real charity in the Christian sense of the word. It is given grudgingly. It excites no
gratitude in the recipient. Its administration is, at the
best, costly and clumsy, and is not attended by the religious and moral advantages which are the privileges and
rewards of spontaneous individual beneficence.

Dr. Chalmers' testimony as to the condition of some
unassessed parishes of Scotland, where a Christian system

of relief was practised, is a striking one :—" The relative affections seem to be in much more powerful exercise in the unassessed than in the assessed parishes ; as also the kindness of neighbours to each other, and the spontaneous generosity of the rich to the poor. There is a great deal of relief going on in the unassessed parishes—perhaps as much in point of *matériel* as in the assessed ; *though not so much needed, from the unbroken habits of economy and industry among the people.* The *morale* which accompanies the voluntary mode of relief tends to sweeten and cement the parochial society in the unassessed parishes."

Dr. Chalmers, Dr. Campbell (of London), and others have urged the Christian Churches to take the care of the poor much more upon themselves than is now the case, and in particular to secure a provision for their *aged* poor. Till this course is adopted, the poor-laws are a necessary evil to avoid a worse result. But if all Churches had acted like the Friends, there would be no need of such laws for the maintenance of the poor.

As to the third great practical characteristic of Quakerism—its provision of a liberal education for every youthful member of its community—there can be little question but that no other denomination whatever has ever approached it in this respect. Every Friend (poor as well as rich) may be enabled to secure to his offspring a good *boarding-school education.* The question of "middle-class education" has been long ago solved by the Friends in addition to that of the instruction of their poor. Hence the source of a large amount of the morality, intelligence, influence and general prosperity, which characterise the Friends as a body; hence, in great degree, the small amount of privation amongst them; hence also, in part, the fact that Friends so exceedingly seldom come under the care of the police or the magistracy.

When it is remembered that the total number of Friends in Great Britain and Ireland barely amounts to 15,000 (far fewer than could be contained in the Agricultural Hall at Islington), the provision made for the education of their offspring is marvellous.

In addition to day-schools and private tutors, there are more than twenty private boarding-schools (with terms ranging from thirty-five to one hundred guineas per annum for each scholar), supported almost exclusively by the well-to-do classes of Friends. Of these, the one at Tottenham stands at the head, being the Eton or Rugby of Quakerism, and devoted entirely to the education of the sons of the wealthier Friends.

In addition to these twenty private schools, there are twelve *public* boarding-schools for the Society. The latter are under the control of committees appointed by the Friends, and are more or less subsidised by annual subscriptions or permanent endowments, so as to be enabled to furnish a good education to the children of the middle-class and poorer Friends, at a charge very much below cost price. These twelve public schools are respectively situated at Ackworth, near Pontefract; Croydon, near London; Sidcot, near Bristol; Wigton, near Carlisle; Rawden, near Leeds; Penketh, near Warrington; Sibford, near Banbury; Ayton, near Middlesboro'; Waterford, Mountmellick, Lisburn, and Brookfield near Belfast. They contain, on an average, nearly 1,000 boarders in the aggregate.

The same twelve schools have permanent endowments of the value of more than one hundred and fifty thousand pounds, and receive annual subscriptions to the extent of about £5,500. In addition, the payments received annually for each pupil average £14 per head.

Not included in the above list is a training college for gratuitously educating teachers, named the Flounders Institute, after its founder, Benjamin Flounders, a Liverpool merchant, who endowed it with £40,000. It is in Yorkshire, near the Society's large public school of Ackworth. Many of the students of this institution and of the elder pupils of Tottenham School subsequently graduate at the University of London, and often with considerable distinction.

In all the Friends' schools (especially the public ones) the useful and practical branches of study are mainly cultivated, and very little attention is devoted to merely ornamental attainments. The study of the classics is made a prominent one in several of the principal Quaker institutions, but by no means to the exclusion of the pursuits likely to be required in ordinary business life. In the girls' schools, "the accomplishments" are, comparatively, slighted. Just a little music is taught, but no dancing. The Quaker girls are early trained to habits of usefulness and industry. In after life they are required to aid the men in the administration of the charitable and educational functions of the Society, so far at least as their own sex is concerned. Thus many of the female Friends acquire much skill in many matters of business and of executive philanthropy, which renders them less dependent on men than the ladies of most other denomi-

nations are. A large number of the young men and
women in the Friends' Society devote their Sabbaths to
the gratuitous instruction of the children of their poorer
neighbours of other sects, or of no sect at all.

This recent " Sabbath-school movement" amongst the
Friends has exerted a remarkable influence in stirring
up the Society, and especially its youthful members, to
religious earnestness. This must be evident when we
remember, that out of this body of 15,000 persons,
nearly 1,000 (elder and younger) devote a considerable
portion of the Sabbath (and often of week-days also) to
the self-denying and always gratuitous work of teaching
the poorest, most squalid, and most ignorant of the
juvenile and adult population around them. For this
noble work the Society is, under God, indebted in great
degree to the energetic example and efforts of Joseph
Storrs Fry and Arthur Naish, of Bristol, and William
White, of Birmingham.

The Society thus supports about seventy-five Sabbath-
schools, and (by means of 960 teachers) educates 11,000
pupils in them. It is a very noteworthy circumstance,
that scarcely a single pupil amongst these is a Friend,
and very few indeed ever become united to the Society,
although the kind care of these Quaker teachers is highly
valued both by the scholars and their parents.

This matter is associated with a further characteristic
of the Society, viz. that it is practically not a proselytising
body. Notwithstanding the many excellent qualities of
the Friends and the peculiarly liberal nature of most of
their arrangements, they are (often to their own astonishment and regret) found to be practically one of the most

exclusive sects in Christendom. Notwithstanding their unsurpassed charity to the poor and the peculiarly democratic nature of their arrangements, they are in some respects a most aristocratic body. Thus, in going into a Quaker meeting, one seldom sees any attenders from the really indigent and ignorant masses of the nation. Most things about the Quaker assemblies are so "respectable," so systematised, so well looked after, so toned down to quietude, order, and harmony, that only the initiated, the habitual Friends, can, as a rule, settle comfortably and advantageously into all the usual arrangements. Then the pecuniary and educational privileges of membership are so many, that a constant vigilance is requisite to avoid the reception of candidates for admission who may be prompted by interested motives. And, again, there is the extent to which the Friends, owing to their small aggregate number, their education after one general plan, and their habitual disciplinary and social intercourse, acquire the class feeling of a social brotherhood or of a large religious benefit club; and all this makes strangers feel still more strange and uncongenial than they would otherwise be. Further, the religious and doctrinal views of the Friends are so extreme on some points, so different from those of other sects, that outsiders feel themselves, on casually entering a Quaker company, in a totally different atmosphere from what they have been accustomed to, and one which requires long training to get used to. No man can become a Friend in a hurry. And, indeed, it may be generally asserted that Quakerism, in its essence and actuality, is not at all adapted for the masses of mankind. It is rather a very excellent, but very eclectic, system, suited only for the more thoughtful and serious of Christians, and for persons with minds disciplined to deep feelings and abstract contemplation, and with strong preferences for individual freedom of religious action. Thomas Carlyle has, we believe, somewhere written that "the United Kingdom contains a population of thirty million people, the major part whereof are fools." This humorous libel has in it a fraction of truth, in so far as that a very large proportion of mankind (whether English or others) do not wish to think for themselves. They do not desire to be independent of other men's control in religious matters. They are neither wishful nor able to exercise their spirits in earnest strivings for a realisation of close communion with their invisible Lord. If caring little about any religion, they rather covet the easy quietude of being able to feel that they can lay their religious cares and responsibilities upon other shoulders than their own. They shrink with disinclination, if not with repulsion, from uniting themselves with a community not only requiring a very strict discipline as to morals, and exercising a vigilant but brotherly scrutiny over the actions of its members, but also refusing to recognise a corporate responsibility for each individual conscience and life.

Hence few men are likely to seek communion with the Society of Friends. And practically, the Friends seldom gain converts, or at least adherents. Perhaps it is not to be desired that they should gain many, as mankind are now constituted; for if the Society were swamped with a mass of converts not prepared to enter fully into the spirit of its communion, the tone of the whole body

would be lowered, and possibly its constitution become
radically altered. The Quakers are a select and disciplined
body, better qualified for influencing outsiders than for
uniting with them in permanent communion. They have
exercised very great influence on the surrounding world;
far more, in proportion to their very small number, than
any other sect that ever existed—the Jesuits not excepted.
But the retention of this beneficial influence is only compatible with their maintenance of the strict discipline and high
morality of their body. This would hardly be practicable
with any considerable accession of persons not prepared
for the abstract views and decided principles of the Society.

During the past quarter of a century, the Friends in
the United Kingdom have sent their preachers to the
most remote parts of the world; to Hindostan, the Pacific
Islands, Australia, New Zealand, the Cape Colony, the
West Indies, California, Greenland, Iceland, Russia, the
Faroe Islands, Lapland, Madagascar, Egypt, Syria, and
the Holy Land. These good men have preached assiduously to a vast number of audiences; have given cheering
counsel to the resident missionaries of other denominations; have administered considerable pecuniary relief
to the necessitous, and have disseminated innumerable
publications relative to Quaker doctrine. It is to be
hoped that all these efforts, necessarily involving an
expense of many thousand pounds, have been attended
with good to many souls, and have deepened the faith
and increased the Christian knowledge of the persons thus
visited. But it is pretty certain that no appreciable
accession to the numbers of the Friends has ever resulted
in consequence.

In addition to all this, Quaker ministers are continually traversing the various counties of the United Kingdom, holding meetings to which the public are invited, distributing tracts which inculcate their doctrines, and in other ways attempting to promulgate their views. These attempts are received with general satisfaction; nevertheless it is, at best, but an exceedingly small number of outsiders who become in consequence members of the Society. For instance, one of the most active of Quaker home-missionaries has been a zealous, excellent gentleman, named Jonathan Grubb, who has for years laboured assiduously in preaching to the poor, especially in the rural districts of Suffolk, Essex, and Norfolk. His meetings have been largely attended, and have also been occasions of much solemnity and tenderness of spirit. They have often been followed up by sympathising private conversations with some of the most impressed amongst the hearers. Great religious edification has doubtless ensued in consequence. But we have not heard of any fresh accessions to the ranks of Quakerism from any or all of these meetings.

More than two hundred years ago a Quaker boy named James Parnell, some sixteen years of age, often bigoted in his views and addresses, preached vigorously to the people of the same Eastern Counties, and gathered in hundreds and probably thousands to the fold of his people in the very district where Mr. Grubb (a man far superior to young Parnell in most Christian virtues) can barely secure one proselyte in several years' ministerial activity. In that Eastern District the Quaker ranks are now becoming smaller and smaller. For instance, their congregations at Norwich and Ipswich, notwithstanding they have contained some of the most influential and worthy persons in the vicinity, have for years been sadly dwindling. Thus Norwich, which about forty years ago contained five hundred Friends, has now barely thirty.

It thus appears that the Quaker system is an admirable one for developing a small band of active, independent, philanthropic, and spiritual Christians, but fails most decidedly in gathering in the masses of mankind. This is now generally admitted by the Friends. One of them, an aged minister, lately remarked to the writer, " Well, I must confess that if the evangelisation of the great body of the people had depended upon us, very little would have been done." It would appear that, in aiming at perfection, the Friends have arrived at many conclusions incompatible with the actual constitution of imperfect and frail humanity. It is often observed that in the communication of religious instruction to the poor, a rough and ready, but comparatively uneducated, yet zealous, working-man is far more effective than a calm, refined, and highly-educated speaker. Similarly, the very agencies which the Friends deprecate and avoid as imperfect, namely, " the one man system," hearty congregational singing, untrammelled zealous preaching, outwardly visible sacraments, settled pastorates and paid ministries, these or other such arrangements are evidently and practically essential to the evangelisation of the *great masses of mankind*, in spite of all the arguments of Quakerism and notwithstanding the admirable results (on a very limited scale) of a system from which these agencies have been almost entirely excluded.

c

Hence, when the Friend pleads for his distinctive religious system, his auditor—whether Catholic, Episcopalian, Presbyterian, Methodist, or Congregationalist—may fairly reply, "Yes, all that you say is very good. Your arguments are reasonable up to a certain point. Your conclusions follow logically from some selections of Scripture texts. But, notwithstanding all this, you lack a crowning argument, that afforded by the adaptability of any religious system to gather in the great multitudes of mankind to the fold of Gospel fellowship. Here you fail, and fail enormously. You are a first-rate sect for the *further development of some ready-made Christians*, but your arrangements are not suited to work up the raw material of home and foreign paganism, unless perhaps in a few exceptional cases.

"It is known that your organisers, Fox and others, gathered their followers almost exclusively from the already converted Puritans, and especially from the Baptists. Whenever you have tried to build on *your own foundations*, you have had scarcely any success. You can sometimes reap the choicest crops of other men's Christian husbandry; but small indeed are the harvests wherever you have been the first sowers of the Gospel seed. In short, your Quaker system is like a dish of religious confectionery, well adapted to richly feast a few, but unsuited for the purpose of furnishing with plain, rough, healthy fare the great tables needed to satisfy the multitudes of spiritually starving humanity."

In further reply the Friend may urge some such defence as this: "Whilst it is true that we are a very small sect, and that we do not gather others largely into our fold, we have

been able to promote the usefulness of members of other
denominations to a much more considerable extent than is
popularly supposed. If we do not evangelise the masses
directly, we do so, in great degree, *indirectly*. For,
by our peculiar zeal and success in promoting the spread of
popular education and temperance; by our large pecuniary aid to tract societies and home missions; by our
universally acknowledged supremacy in exertions to eman-
cipate millions of enslaved fellow-creatures; by our
special activity in securing useful political reforms for the
masses of our countrymen; by these and other similar
means, we have probably done as much for the present and
eventual advantage of the great body of the people (as to
moral and spiritual progress) as the whole of the Anglican Church has ever done with its enormous revenues,
State patronage, and ten or fifteen millions of real and
nominal adherents. Indeed, we have probably done far
more by our fifteen thousand than the Anglican Church by
its millions. Show us, if you can, the names of princely-
paid prelates who have done as much for the oppressed
slaves as our plain untitled Quakers have, or who have
laboured as we have in the great works of temperance and
peace, in prison and penal amelioration, and other extensive
moral and social reforms. Have we not, indeed, sometimes
had direct opposition, and the most contumelious and
unchristian contempt manifested toward us by these clergy,
instead of their hearty co-operation in our works of Christian
charity and world-wide usefulness? Further, we have always
tolerated the opinions of others. No brand of fierce persecution has distinguished our sect—(alas, that we are
almost alone in this respect!) Even when we have had

c 2

power to punish our opponents we have repeatedly and
uniformly shown Christian forbearance. If, in short, we
have not succeeded as to the number and quantity of our
adherents, we have been enabled to maintain a corporate
standard of Christian life and action unsurpassed by any;
and, therefore, beneficial in its example to all the surrounding sects, and to the millions of outsiders also. It is not,
perhaps, given to any denominations to excel at the same
time in quantity *and* quality. For instance, look at the
Moravian Church, which has long held up a pure and holy
beacon-light of humble Christian discipleship and pre-
eminent missionary zeal—that ancient church which no
sect of Christendom can claim to surpass, if equal, in
fidelity to its Lord, and which has especially stood forth for
the three fundamental principles that the Holy Scriptures
in their simplicity, apart from all articles or creeds, are
the sufficient source of Christian instruction; that the
exceeding preciousness of the Redeemer's atoning blood is
to be prominently and constantly cherished and set forth;
and that it should be the daily effort of each Christian to
live reverently and humbly, as being in the very sight of
the personal Lord Jesus in heaven, invisible but (through
the medium of His Spirit, dispensed to each) perceiving
every act and thought, and ultimately rewarding each
in His future kingdom, when He will again be visibly
revealed to His people. Look at that small but honoured
sect. They are stated to have *only five thousand adherents*
in great Britain, another five thousand in Germany, and
a somewhat larger number in America. But who can
estimate their quiet but great influence in the world? In
like manner, the influence of the Society of Friends on the

world at large must not be merely estimated by the number
of its visible adherents.   On the contrary, it is probable
that if it is faithful to its best principles of Christian
service, its numbers will become yet smaller, comparatively,
whilst the more extended will be its real and beneficent,
though sometimes invisible, influence in Christendom."

We have here supposed our Friend to speak for his sect
with less reticence than modesty would permit any
individual Christian to allude to his own personal efforts
or influence.

But, in confirmation of the above defence of the Friends
on the ground of their peculiar influence upon the
world, in indirect and direct ways, let us just glance at
the most prominent philanthropic and other beneficent
movements of the past two or three generations, and
it will be at once seen, that those movements have derived
an extraordinary advantage from Quaker leaders, beyond
all proportion to the very limited extent of the Society.

First, on reviewing the great *Anti-Slavery contest*, how
prominent have been the names of Friends : as for instance,
Joseph Sturge, William Allen, William Forster, Josiah
Forster, Joseph Cooper, Thomas Harvey, Joseph John
Gurney, Wilson Armistead, Joseph Gurney Bevan, George
W. Alexander, Richard Davis Webb, the Croppers, and
others.   Clarkson was greatly prompted and sustained in
his labours by Friends.   Sir Thomas Fowell Buxton also
was largely indebted for his success to the aid derived from
J. J. Gurney, and others of the Society.   Lord Brougham
received similar energetic and most valuable (though often
unobserved) co-operation from Quaker abolitionists (especially from William Allen of Lombard Street).

On the other side the Atlantic, the Quaker poet Whittier for many years animated the small band of Abolitionists with persevering energy by the clarion notes of his soul-stirring muse. Some of the most earnest and enlivening appeals for freedom ever penned, have originated with this plain and quiet Friend. The originator and chief sustainer of the celebrated "Underground Railway" in America—that is, the systematic plan for facilitating the transit of escaped slaves across the State of Ohio to the British possessions—was a Friend, Levi Coffin, of Cincinnati (depicted in "Uncle Tom's Cabin" as "Simeon Halliday"). Through his instrumentality alone many thousand slaves were safely concealed and transmitted beyond the power of their cruel owners and pursuers.

Since the termination of the American civil war, and the abolition of slavery there, the Society of Friends in Great Britain and the United States has made extraordinary efforts for the relief, education, and permanent training of the four millions of Freedmen thus suddenly emancipated. Nearly £200,000 (or about half the total relief contributed for the assistance of the Freedmen) has been raised by the Friends alone from their own members. Amongst those who have worked in this cause Friends have been in the foremost rank, especially Arthur Albright, the Cadburys, and other Birmingham Friends, William and Stafford Allen, Smith Harrison, Robert Alsop, John Hodgkin, Frederick Seebohm, Joseph Simpson, John Taylor, George Thomas (of Bristol), and Robert Charleton.

In the United States these English Friends have been *vigorously* co-operated with in their efforts by the Transatlantic members of the confraternity ; especially by Levi Coffin, Charles F. Coffin, and Timothy Harrison (of Richmond, Ind.), Murray Shipley, Francis T. King (of Baltimore), William F. Mitchell (of Tennessee), Elkanah Beard, and others. General Howard, the excellent president of the United States' official " Freedmen's Bureau," has repeatedly sought the aid, and followed the counsels, of the Friends in this philanthropic work, which he has so efficiently promoted.

When, on the sudden failure of the potato crop, *the Irish famine* brought multitudes face to face with starvation and death, none more vigorously flew to the rescue than the Friends. William Forster, Joseph Bewley, Samuel Bewley, Richard Allen, Jonathan Pim, and many others, entered heart and soul into the leadership of that work of mercy. Many thousands of pounds were speedily raised by the 15,000 Quakers, and their own agents visited the most famished districts, and personally superintended the administration of relief.

During late years there have been several severe *famines in Finland.* The relief of these starving people has been specially undertaken by some of the Friends, and in particular by the Sturges and Bakers of Birmingham, William Pollard of Hertford, the Gibsons of Saffron Walden, and John Good of Hull.

In the promotion of the work of *Popular Education*, the British and Foreign School Society (with which the Quaker names of Joseph Lancaster and William Allen are prominently connected, and which was mainly instituted and sustained by Friends) has exerted a wide-spread and very useful influence.

In their general advocacy of *the Peace Question* the Friends have been pre-eminent. They have not only endured innumerable fines and imprisonments for refusing to fight, but have laboriously sought to promulgate their views of the unlawfulness of war amongst other denominations. In this work the names of Joseph Tregelles Price (of Neath), Joseph and Charles Sturge, Joseph Pease, Henry Pease, Edmund Fry, Samuel Gurney (elder and younger), Robert Charleton, John Priestman (of Bradford), Edward Smith and William Hargreaves (of Sheffield), William Rowntree, Frederic Wheeler, and others are well known.

The efforts for *the Amelioration of the Penal Code* and *the Improvement of Prison Discipline* made by the Friends have been unsurpassed by any other denomination. Here again, the names of Joseph John Gurney, Elizabeth Fry, Peter Bedford, John Thomas Barry, John Bright, Charles Gilpin, Alfred Dymond, Joseph Spence, Josiah and William Forster, the Sparkses, William Rathbone, Joseph Gurney* Barclay, the Allens, Peases, George Thomas, and others, have been foremost. Of Barry alone, it may be said that, working silently, and for the most part in secret, (by influencing other men more powerful and prominent than himself,) he was more instrumental in the successive repeals of the death-penalty for various offences, in the interval from 1829-40, than any other man in the kingdom. Of course he could not have done what he did but for the co-operation of others, especially Members of Parliament like William Ewart, and journalists like John Sydney Taylor. These two gentlemen were not Friends, but were constantly and greatly helped by Quaker support.

The first great movement for the *Health of Towns* and *Sanitary Reform* was mainly supported by Friends, especially by the munificent Joseph Eaton of Bristol, a man who, whilst living in a very small house, in the simplest style, devoted nearly all his income to works of usefulness and charity. Thus, on one occasion during his lifetime, he presented £5,000 to a local hospital.

In the efforts of the *Bible Society* the Friends have, in proportion to their numbers, been in no wise behindhand. Where their tongues have not spoken, their hands and purses have aided. A Friend, Richard Phillips, was one of the founders of this noble association. The Quaker names of William Forster, Josiah Forster, Thomas Norton and Thomas Binns, are well known amongst the most steadily useful of the members of the central committee of that association.

For *local and miscellaneous philanthropy*, Quaker names are everywhere held in honour, especially such as Richard Reynolds of Bristol, James Cropper of Liverpool, Peter Bedford of Spitalfields and Croydon, Edward Thomas of Bristol, George Bradshaw and Isaac Wright of Manchester, Richard Dykes Alexander of Ipswich, John Allen of Liskeard, Joseph Rowntree of York, Joseph Bewley of Dublin, Edward Pease of Darlington, George Richardson of Newcastle, William Tanner of Bristol, John Baker of Thirsk, Joseph Sturge of Birmingham, Isaac Braithwaite of Kendal, Robert Ransome of Ipswich, Edward Hallam of Axbridge, William Forster of Tottenham, Dr. Hodgkin of London, and John Yeardley of Stamford Hill. All these good men are deceased, but they have many living representatives in their own little community. The names of many "honourable women" might be added to this list, such as the late Elizabeth Fry of London, Ann Alexander of York, Ann Alexander of Ipswich, Louisa Radley of Tottenham, Philippa Williams of Redruth, and a host of other "sisters of charity," all "gone home," but succeeded too by others like-hearted.

The Quaker philanthropists of America are also of honoured reputation; as for instance, Anthony Benezet of Philadelphia, Elijah Coffin of Indiana, Stephen Grellet of New Jersey, Isaac Collins of Philadelphia, Dr. S. B. Tobey of Rhode Island, and Isaac T. Hopper of New York.

In the stirring world of politics the 15,000 have been fully represented. In each Parliament there are generally from four to six Friends, and these have never been men of less than respectable M.P. ability. The name of one Quaker, John Bright, towers high above the general level of contemporary statesmen, attaining to the first rank of celebrity for talent, eloquence, incorruptibility, boldness, and consistency, and in no wise behind the reputation of Hampden, Peel, Pitt, Fox, Russell, Aberdeen, Brougham, Wilberforce, or Gladstone. His friend, Richard Cobden *(par nobile fratrum)*, though not a Quaker, was largely imbued with Quaker sentiments, and was zealously and persistently supported by the political partizanship of members of that denomination. Amongst other useful Quaker legislators are the names of Joseph Pease, Henry Pease, Whitwell Pease, Charles Gilpin, Jonathan Pim, John Ellis, Samuel Gurney, E. A. Leatham, W. H. Leatham, and Jacob Bright. (William Edward Forster,

M.P. for Bradford, and James Wilson, Chancellor of Exchequer for India, were once Quakers.)

Measures of sterling worth, calculated to promote the real advancement of the British people, have found amongst Quaker politicians, whether in or out of Parliament, some of their most hearty co-operators. In particular, the great *Anti-Corn Law League* was vigorously supported by Friends.

In *Science and Literature* the Friends have not been so prominent as in other good things; but even here they are not without useful contributors to progress. Dr. Dalton, the discoverer of the atomic theory, was a Quaker. So was Dr. Thomas Young, the interpreter of Egyptian hieroglyphics, &c. Robert Were Fox, F.R.S., of Falmouth, has done much for the elucidation of the formation of mineral deposits. Joseph Jackson Lister, F.R.S., of Upton, is a name well known in the history of microscopic and optical discovery. Professor Oliver of Kew, James Backhouse, sen. and jun., of York, Edward Newman of London, Gough, "the blind botanist," Henry E. Brady of Newcastle, and John Gilbert Baker of Thirsk and Kew, have acquired honour amongst botanists. Luke Howard, F.R.S., Isaac Fletcher, Isaac Brown, Principal of the Flounders Institute, Samuel Marshall of Kendal, and Lovell Squire of Falmouth, have rendered good service to meteorological science. William Pengelly of Torquay is one of the most active of provincial geologists. Alfred Tylor of London has also aided the progress of this and kindred sciences. George Stephenson was greatly indebted to the patronage of a Quaker—Edward Pease—of Darlington, for his development of the English railway system. The ingenious

contrivance for stamping and numbering railway tickets—
as used daily and hourly at every railway station—was
the invention of a Friend, named Edmondson we believe.
The development of the china clay deposits of Cornwall,
and their application to the porcelain manufactures, was
largely owing to a Quaker, William Cookworthy of
Plymouth.

In *medicine*, the Quaker physicians have often acquired
eminence; as for instance, Dr. Fothergill, Dr. Lettsom,
Dr. Pope, the favourite attendant of King George III.,
Dr. Wilson Fox, Dr. Rutty, Dr. Thomas Hodgkin, and
Dr. Peacock.

In the *treatment of the Insane*, the Friends and their
" Retreat " at York have an honourable reputation, especially William Tuke, Dr. Daniel Tuke, Dr. Caleb Williams,
and Dr. Kitching.

The Quaker poets are also few; but Bernard Barton,
Alaric A. Watts, Thomas Lister, Mary Howitt, Elizabeth
B. Prideaux, Wm. Ball, T. Frederic Ball, and Hannah
Bowden, have all written with much taste and feeling.
Mrs. Opie, Mrs. Ellis (Sarah Stickney), Mary Lead-
beater, Mary Ann Kelty, A. Letitia Waring, Maria Hack,
Maria Webb, Henrietta J. Fry, Frances Prideaux, authoress
of " Claudia," and E. J. Tuckett are Quaker authoresses,
whose works possess considerable interest. Lindley
Murray's name as a grammarian is known everywhere.
The theological writings of Joseph John Gurney; the
interesting biographies of S. Grellet and William Forster,
by Benjamin Seebohm; the Commentaries, &c. by Dr.
Edward Ash of Bristol; Edward Tylor's " Anahuac ;" S.
Capper's " Acknowledged Doctrines ;" the Spanish trans-

lations, &c., by J. J. Wiffen; C. Tylor's "Franconia;" the valuable work on Ireland by Jonathan Pim; Dymond's "Essays on Morality;" and Wilson Armistead's anti-slavery works, have all attracted considerable attention outside the circle of Quakerism. Francis Fry of Bristol, and Anthony Purver, are Quaker names well known to students of Biblical literature. Frederic Seebohm's work on "The Oxford Reformers"—originally appearing in the *Fortnightly Review*—has taken its place amongst the standard historical works of the age. A Friend, Martin Wood, edits the *Times of India*. In Great Britain the Society supports a quarterly review, the *Friends' Examiner*, edited by William C. Westlake; and two monthlies —the *Friend*, edited by John Frank, and the *British Friend*, edited by Robert Smeal. A catalogue of exclusively Quaker literature, filling 2,011 closely-printed pages, has recently been compiled by Joseph Smith (London, 1867). So that, after all, these names are not a very scanty contribution to the world of science and literature from a little band of 15,000.

In the work of *City Missions*, the Friends have of very recent years taken an active part, especially in the Metropolis; where the Bedford Institute at Spitalfields—named after the well-known Peter Bedford*—is a nucleus for a number of philanthropic efforts—schools, workmen's club, dispensary, invalid kitchen, mothers' meetings, &c.—for the welfare of the poor of East London. Edmund Pace, John G. Hine, William Beck, and others, manage its operations with success.

* See "Peter Bedford, the Spitalfields Philanthropist." London: S. W. Partridge & Co. Price 2s. 6d.

Similar efforts are made in other large towns; as at
Birmingham, by William White, John Edward Wilson,
&c.; at Liverpool by B. Townson, T. Crosfield, &c.; and
elsewhere.

The great *Temperance Movement*, which has done so
much towards the moral and social progress of our country,
has had a large proportion of Quaker leaders; amongst
whom may be especially named Thomas Shillitoe, Joseph
Eaton, Richard Barrett, William Janson, Richard Dykes
Alexander of Ipswich, Nathaniel Card and Charles
Thompson of Manchester, the Peases of Darlington,
George Thomas, and Robert Charleton of Bristol, the
Cadburys of Birmingham and Banbury, Edward Back-
house of Sunderland, the Clarks of Street, Joseph Spence
of York, Joseph Thorp of Halifax, Edward Smith of
Sheffield, Samuel Bowly of Gloucester, Henry Russell of
Dublin, John Taylor of London, Jonathan Grubb of
Sudbury, and Edward Hornor of Halstead.

The movement for supplying public *Drinking Fountains*
in cities and towns has had for its leader a Friend, Samuel
Gurney, M.P., and other members of the Society as its
prominent supporters.

The *Aborigines' Protection Society* has been mainly
carried on by Friends and ex-Friends, and in particular
by Dr. Hodgkin, Robert N. Fowler, Robert Alsop, and
James Bell.

In the great world of *Commerce* and *Enterprise* the
Society of Friends have taken a prominently useful part.
Their bankers and merchants have maintained, with very
rare exceptions, a conspicuously honourable and just
position. In looking over the list of English bankers.

the number of Quaker names is very striking for so
extremely small a community. Amongst these are those
of the Barclays, Gurneys, Alexanders, Fowlers, Drewetts,
and Dimsdales of Lombard Street and Cornhill (the
Hoares and Hanburys were once Friends), the Peases and
Backhouses of Durham, the Sharples, Tukes, and Lucases
of Hertfordshire, the Gibsons of Saffron Walden, the
Alexanders of Ipswich, the Crewdsons of Kendal, the
Spences of Newcastle, the Lloyds of Birmingham, the
Hutchinsons and Ellises of Leicester, the Heads and
Mounseys of Carlisle, the Bassetts of Leighton Buzzard,
the Foxes, Williamses, and Tweedys of Cornwall, the
Leathams of West Yorkshire, the Gilletts of Banbury,
the Peckovers of Wisbeach, the Ashbys of Staines, and
others, to say nothing of the numerous Quaker directors
of joint-stock banks. These houses have obtained long
and well-merited public confidence. Quaker names are
also well known on railway boards. The few lines of
railway where Quaker directors have had the upper hand
have been managed with much success; for instance, the
Stockton and Darlington. Bradshaw's Railway Guide
was originated by a Friend.

The Quaker Insurance Companies, including the
Friends' Provident, the United Kingdom, the National
Provident, and the Metropolitan—all largely managed by
Friends—continue to be specially successful and safe.

The Quaker Steam Packet Companies include those of
the Malcomsons of London, Liverpool, Dublin, and
Waterford, and of the Pikes of Cork, probably larger
and better managed fleets of steamers than possessed by
any other company not subsidised by Government. The

Tindalls, the Wilsons of Sunderland, the Thompsons, Grimshaws, and Nicholsons of Liverpool, are well known amongst shipowners.

In many other branches of commerce and trade Quaker prominence is striking; for instance, the Ashworths, Brights, Emmotts, Kings, Braithwaites, Priestmans, Thomassons, Hodgkinsons, Holdsworths, Naishes, Ecroyds, Burgesses, Rices, Cashes, Pims, Richardsons, and Malcomsons amongst the textile manufacturing firms; the Frys, Cadburys, and Rowntrees in the chocolate business; the Ransomes, Mays, Sims, Fowlers, Hewitsons, Tangyes, Whitwells, Worsdells, Gilkes, Wilsons, Tylors, and Warners in general engineering and the manufacture of agricultural instruments; the Darbys and Dickensons of the Colebrookdale Ironworks; Hargreaves, Smiths, and others in cutlery; Huntley and Palmer, Carr, Haylock, and Slater in the wholesale manufacture of biscuits; the Hanburys, Allens, Corbyns, Howards, and Warners as manufacturing chemists; the Reckitts in the starch trade; Bryant and May, and Tylor and Pace as wholesale manufacturers of matches and safety lights; Williams, Foster and Co. as copper-ore merchants; Henry Bath and Sons of Swansea, perhaps the largest British consignees of foreign copper and silver; the Hornimans, Harrisons, and Crosfields in the tea trade; the Christys and Coopers as hat manufacturers; the Crowleys of Alton and Croydon, the Ashbys of Staines, and the Lucases of Hitchin, as brewers.

The Cornish and other mines have been largely worked by the Friends, especially by the Fox family of Falmouth, and the Williamses of Redruth. The Sturges of Birming-

ham and Gloucester, and other Friends, are amongst the
leading men in the corn trade.

Many further Quaker names might be mentioned as
holding a respectable and prominent position in the
various branches of trade and commerce.

But the position collectively occupied by those above
named—especially the ones prominent in philanthropy
and social progress — is doubtless unequalled by any
similar number of names that can be collected from any
body of merely 15,000 persons. Many small kingdoms,
or states of several million inhabitants, do not exercise so
wide an influence upon the world as do these few Quakers.

The influence of Quakerism in the United States has
been less of a personal kind than in Great Britain ; but
the practical principles of the Society have been indirectly
received to a very considerable extent in that large nation.
The Friends were the founders of the State of Pennsylvania, and occupied a prominent position also in the
early governments of Rhode Island, Delaware, and other
colonies. Hence they had opportunities—of which they
availed themselves—for largely moulding the first legis-
lation of those States. To their influence may be mainly
traced the general freedom of the United States from
religious persecutions, from the numerous titles, " blazing
garments," and other semi-barbaric gewgaws of European
courts ; from unduly severe penal codes and unmerciful
treatment of criminals, and from any extensive neglect of
public education, or of provision for the poor.

Through William Penn and his companions, George
Fox has probably exerted even a greater influence upon
the American continent than in Great Britain.

D

There is yet a further manifestation of useful Quaker influence, namely, that exerted through the considerable number of persons who, after having been trained in the habits and general sentiments of the sect, have, from various causes, afterwards quitted its fold for some other section of the universal Church. To most of these, the remark, " once a Quaker, always a Quaker," applies with even more force than the proverbs, " once a priest, always a priest," "once a Jesuit, always a Jesuit." For, any person once imbued with the active, independent habit of mind which Quaker training peculiarly fosters, can rarely, if ever, divest himself of it. The old feelings of untransferable individual responsibility, philanthropic interest, and cautious examination, continually assert themselves in the ex-Friends. Hence, Quakers who join the ranks of Episcopalianism, Unitarianism, Plymouth Brethrenism, &c. often become specially earnest and valuable members of these denominations.

For instance, amongst such worthy examples we may name the following ex-Friends : William Rathbone, of Liverpool, William Edward Forster, M.P. for Bradford, Henry Bewley of Dublin, William and Mary Howitt, Mrs. Sarah Ellis of Hoddesdon, Richard Davis Webb of Dublin, Frederic Lucas, Robert N. Fowler of London, Isaac B. Cooke of Liverpool, the Crewdsons, Wilsons, Croppers, and Wakefields of Kendal, Isaac Crewdson of Manchester, Potto Brown of Earith, John Cropper of Liverpool, and many others.

The following and other well-known persons were either of Quaker birth or descent, viz. Lord Lyndhurst ; Lord Gough ; Dr. Tregelles, the Biblical scholar ; Dr. Birch, tutor to the Prince of Wales; Dr. Pritchard, author of the *Unity of the Human Race;* Rickman, the ecclesiastical architect; Boulton, the coadjutor of James Watt; Francis Galton, natural philosopher; Dr. Birkbeck, founder of Mechanics' Institutes; John Harford of Blaize Castle, author; Professor Joseph Lister of Glasgow; Sir Henry Rawlinson, decipherer of cuneiform inscriptions; John H. Gurney, naturalist; Ward, the Indian missionary; Professor William A. Miller, chemist; Professor W. H. Harvey, botanist; and Professor W. Neilson Hancock, LL.D., statistician and political economist.

The Hon. Neal Dow of Portland, Maine, to whom New England is indebted for the " Maine Liquor Law," was born a Quaker, and virtually remains such in many respects.

It is but fair to add to these honourable ex-Quaker names an ignoble exception, Thomas Paine, the infidel writer, whose parents were Friends. But he used for evil purposes the energy and independence of spirit fostered by his early training. In his case, as in that of others, the perversion of the best things ended in the worst results.

The Rev. Joseph Baylee, D.D., the energetic Principal of St. Aidan's Training College, Birkenhead, is an ex-Friend, and, doubtless, his eminent services to the Church of England, are largely owing to his Quaker training. An ex-Friend may more easily become a good clergyman than a tractable lay Episcopalian. He is usually too independent in his habits of thought to "sit under" the authoritative exclusive teaching of any one spiritual guide.

A clergyman complaining bitterly of an ex-Quaker to a friend of the writer, said, "I wish Mr.——had never entered the Church of England. He is always interfering with something—always wanting to exercise his own judgment. He has given me a deal of trouble, and I heartily wish he had never quitted your communion." It is because Friends, as a body, love to "exercise their own judgment," that they have been peculiarly hostile to all spiritual restrictions. Hence too, in politics, there are not many Quaker Tories. There are just a few. As a body, the Friends are Liberals, rather than Radicals.

Much Quaker blood ran in Lord Macaulay's veins, and also, we believe, in those of Sir Walter Scott and Abraham Lincoln. Many of the prominent politicians and soldiers of the United States have been Quakers by birth, or near descent, as, for example, Mr. Secretary Stanton.

The influence of the ex-Quaker element in several districts of England—especially at Manchester, Liverpool, and Kendal—is owing in part to a secession of evangelical Friends about the year 1836, during what was termed the "*Beaconite* Controversy." This originated in the publication of a scriptural and evangelical work, entitled *The Beacon*, written by the late excellent Isaac Crewdson of Manchester, to warn the Friends against the Deistical writings of an American Friend, named Elias Hicks, and at the same time to point out that the root and source of this danger was fairly traceable to deficiencies and errors in the theological writings of George Fox, and still more in those of his associates, Robert Barclay and William Penn. Mr. Crewdson raised as his beacon-cry, "to the Law and to the Testimony," or "Holy Scripture as the alone standard of religious truth." It will hardly be credited by outsiders, now-a-days, that this faithful man and his supporters (numbering several hundred) were compelled to withdraw from the Quaker communion. This was mainly through an unscriptural reverence for the traditions and writings of the early Friends, which, strange to say, had with singular inconsistency pervaded a considerable proportion of their successors. A worthy " elder " of the Lancashire Friends once remarked to the writer—" the best blood of our local Quakerism left us at that sad *Beaconite* controversy."

However, the circumstance has been overruled for good in many ways. The good men who thus quitted Quakerism, transferred their philanthropic and evangelising energies to other sects, (chiefly to the Plymouth Brethren and the Church of England,) and have been widely blessed in their subsequent influence and example. The main body of the Friends—aided especially by the influence of Joseph John Gurney, and the most intelligent and philanthropic men of the Society—have subsequently come round, with little exception, to the very views for which their *Beacon* brethren were obliged to secede.

In reviewing the whole influence of Quakerism, both within and without the Society, it is evident that there must be powerful characteristics, specially operating amongst the Friends, to enable them to acquire such a disproportionate position amongst their fellowmen as they have done. These characteristics are, in particular, those of their universal education, their mutual brotherly watchfulness over each other's conduct, their meditative mode of worship, their union of the social with the religious

element in their large gatherings, and their republican
sense of inalienable individual responsibility to the Lord,
apart from the medium of sacrament or hierarchy.

Further, the man who was the main instrument (under
God) of organising or completing the system of such a
Society, could have been neither the fool nor fanatic that
some of his enemies (including even writers like Lord
Macaulay) have chosen to represent him as being, on
account of certain eccentricities and failings.   He must at
least have possessed rare shrewdness and natural talent ;
(he never received other than the most limited educational
advantages;) and it appears not unreasonable to presume
that he was, in addition, largely endowed with the true
wisdom which comes alone from God, and which is only
granted in special measure to His most humble, obedient,
and prayerful servants.

CHAPTER II.

ANTECEDENTS AND YOUTH OF FOX.

NON-ORIGINALITY OF MUCH OF THE DOCTRINE AND DISCIPLINE
PROMULGATED BY GEORGE FOX—THE STATE CHURCH OF THE
STUARTS—LAUDIAN PERSECUTIONS—THE CIVIL WARS AND
THE PURITANS—CONVENTICLES—PARENTAGE AND EDUCATION
OF GEORGE FOX—SOCIAL ASPECTS OF THE TIMES—FOX'S
YOUTHFUL VIRTUE—EARLY OCCUPATION—LEAVES HOME TO
SEEK FOR RELIGIOUS COUNSEL AND SYMPATHY—FORMATION
OF HIS THEOLOGICAL VIEWS—SOME DEFECTS IN THE LATTER
—FINDS PEACE WITH GOD.

IN the various narratives of the life of George Fox,
and of the rise and establishment of the Society of
Friends, there has been, for the most part, a general non-
recognition of the fact that Quakerism, as respects its
distinguishing *doctrines*, did not originate with the sud-
denness and abruptness that is commonly supposed, as if
it had been a new discovery of truth by Fox, or a revelation
vouchsafed from heaven, for the first time, through his
instrumentality. It appears that there was much more
of steady continuity and successive advance in the progress of the principles of the Reformation towards the
comparatively extreme doctrines of Quakerism than the
Friends themselves have usually recognised. This latter
feature—the non-originality of much of the Quaker
system—has, however, been slightly alluded to in the

valuable and suggestive introduction to a memoir of George Fox, written (it is understood) by Thomas Evans (of Philadelphia) and his brother William. These authors have, to some extent, acknowledged the influence of the Baptists on the subsequent development of the Quaker theology; but the extent of that influence is shown by contemporary records to have been much more considerable than even the Evanses represent it as being.

George Fox, both before and after his entering on the public preaching of the Gospel, associated constantly with the Baptists, from amongst whom, many, if not most, of his first converts were derived. He had an uncle, named Pickering, who was one of that sect; and he mentions in his "Journal" that he visited this uncle, in London, in 1645, about two years before publicly coming forth as a preacher. One of his first sermons was preached at an assembly of Baptists, at Broughton, in Leicestershire, in 1647; and he repeatedly records his intercourse with this denomination throughout his autobiography.

Josiah Marsh, in his interesting Life of Fox, remarks that "the great object of the Reformation was to draw people from the authority of the Church, so called, to the authority of Scripture." But this intelligent writer seems to have greatly overlooked the continuity of the development of these Reformation principles. He does not even mention the Baptists as influencing Quakerism. He briefly alludes, however, to the Brownists and Independents.

The characteristic feature of the Reformation may be further described as the recognition that *men may be safely trusted alone with their Bibles.* The Roman Catholics did not concede this safety. The Lutherans and the

Anglican Church largely, but not fully, admitted it.
The Presbyterians, Brownists, and Independents, carried
on this principle of Christian freedom to successive stages.
The Baptists advanced again in the liberty of private
interpretation, and the Friends have, in some respects at
least, carried it out still farther. But the further process
of this development was a very gradual one, and effected
through much persecution and suffering, especially by the
inflictions endured by the Baptists and the Friends.

It is worthy of notice that whilst the progress of this
fundamental principle of the Reformation was accompanied
in general by a steady proportionate advance of pure and
Apostolic Christianity, the Anglican State Church did
not, in some important respects, improve upon her Roman
sister; but, on the contrary, whilst maintaining a cruel
and most un-Christian system of persecution towards Dissenters, throughout the period of the Stuart sovereigns,
she was lacking in the self-denial, missionary zeal, and
personal holiness, which had for ages adorned many
members of the Roman Church. The character of Archbishop Leighton was indeed an exceedingly beautiful
one; and Usher, Hooker, Taylor, Bedell, and other
Anglicans, were also bright Christian exemplars.

In his " New History of England," G. S. Poulton, after
recognising the most religious and tolerant of the Episcopalians in the eighteenth century—viz. Barrow, Bull,
Cudworth, Leighton, Lightfoot, Pocock, Stillingfleet,
Tillotson, and others, adds : " In all succeeding periods
these illustrious men have been regarded by the Church of
England as her brightest luminaries ; it should be remembered that they were educated and trained *during the*

Commonwealth and under *the tuition and guidance of the Nonconformists Owen and Goodwin,* and others of the same class; and that *many of them were Nonconformists,* until the rigours of this time induced them to conform." (Page 542.)

On the whole an arrogant and unfervent character distinguished the clergy, and especially the dignitaries, of the English State Church, in the interval between the reign of Henry VIII. and that of William III., and, indeed, lasted long after the latter, until at least the stimulus supplied by the rise and rivalry of Methodism in the middle of the eighteenth century. Throughout that long period, the leaders of the Anglican Church, with some exceptions, contrasted very unfavourably with the examples (in preceding ages, or in their own times) of St. Bernard, St. Francis, Thomas à Kempis, Fenelon, Xavier, the Jesuit missionaries of South America, India and Japan; St. Thomas Aquinas, St. Charles Borromeo, St. Bonaventure, St. Philip Neri, St. John of the Cross, St. Theresa, St. Francis Borgia (Duke of Gandia), and other eminently pious Christians of the Roman communion; and again, with such Puritans and Dissenters as Baxter, Manton, Calamy, Bates, Bunyan, Howe, Alleine, Owen, Robinson, Brewster, Skelton, Higgison, Harvard, Mather, Roger Williams, Eliot, Mayhew, Fox, Penn, Burrough, Pennington; the Scotch covenanters, Rutherford, Nielson, McKail, Woodrow, Crawford, John Brown; and a noble army of other like-minded Nonconformists.

How could piety be expected in Bishops selected by an imbecile James the First, or a profligate Charles the Second? The whole history of the seventeenth century is

a most instructive expansion of that notable exclamation
of John Bright: " *The Church religious is one thing; the
Church political is another.*" Very scriptural are (for the
most part) the service, the articles, and the doctrines of
the Church of England. But inseparably associated as
this Church was at that period with unspiritual and
wicked politicians, her excellent teachings were largely
nullified and contradicted by the practical examples
of her professing representatives, who, like a stifling
incubus, pressed her down in the darkness of cruelty
and ungodliness. Thus her doctrines often became
as powerless as the liberal sentiments of a Mexican or
South American constitution, breathing of liberty and
progress *on paper*, but converted into a cruel burlesque
in the hands of irresponsible tyrants. Such was the State
Church of the Stuarts. Happily the modern Anglican
Church has shaken off many of these encumbrances;
but in this, thanks are not due to herself so much as to
the persistent Christian fidelity and stimulating example
of her Nonconformist brethren, who, from the days of
Stuart persecution to the present time, have boldly maintained the necessity for a clearer line of demarcation
between the Church and the world, between the Temple of
God and idols.

This antagonism was the source of Nonconformity in
general, and of Quakerism in particular.

That there was abundant cause for the efforts and active
scruples of the Nonconformists all impartial writers admit;
and this is especially evident from the pages of Church-
men themselves, as Burnet and Pepys. (We once heard
a Quaker remark that " Whoever wishes to understand

many of George Fox's words and actions should first read
Pepys's Diary.")

Lord Macaulay writes of the Laudian period: "Every
little congregation of separatists was tracked out and
broken up. Even the devotions of private families could
not escape the vigilance of Laud's spies. Such fear did
his vigour inspire that the deadly hatred of the Church,
which festered in innumerable bosoms, was generally dis-
guised under an outward show of conformity. On the
very eve of troubles, fatal to himself and to his order, the
Bishops of several extensive dioceses were able to report
to him that not a single Dissenter was to be found within
their jurisdiction."

Laud was of course fully supported in his acts by the
King, who appeared determined to carry into effect the
memorable words of his father James I., when he exclaimed
to the Puritans at Hampton Court, "I will have one
doctrine, one religion, in substance and ceremony, in all
my dominions; so speak no more on that point to me.
No Bishop, no King!" And presently added, with characteristic dignity, "If this be all your party hath to say,
I will make them conform themselves, or else I will harry
them out of the land, or else do worse. No Bishop, no
King!" It was on this occasion that Prelate Bancroft
knelt down before James and exclaimed, "I protest that
my heart melteth for joy that Almighty God of His
singular mercy hath given us such a King as since Christ's
time hath not been." Prelate Whitgift added (with a
strange idea of spiritual "fruits") that "His Majesty
hath assuredly spoken from the Spirit of God."

One of Laud's greatest means of annoying the Puritans

was his attempt to enforce respect to the Book of Sports, that impious work given forth by order of King James, to render, first legal, and then compulsory, the desecration of God's holy Sabbath, and in particular recommending on that day (from the pulpit!) "Sabbath exercises, dancing, archery, leaping, May games, Whitsun ales, morris dances," &c. Some pious bishops and clergymen resisted. These were suspended, imprisoned, or otherwise punished. On the whole, however, the book appears to have had general clerical approval. The Bishop of Bath and Wells had presented Laud with a petition signed by seventy-two of his own clergymen, asking for a restoration of the wakes and revels. He added his belief that "if he had sent for a hundred more, he would have had the consent of them all." Drunkenness, profligacy, and even murder, abundantly followed from this "wickedness in high places" being enforced upon the poor and ignorant. But exceeding pain and scandal ensued amongst the remnant of godly persons in the realm, both Episcopalian and Puritan.

It must be ever borne in mind that there was a true and really Christian Church of Episcopalians at this time, distinct in essence from the political counterfeit styling itself "the Church," although inextricably intertwined with the latter as to its officers and professors. "The Church religious was one thing; the Church political was another." But the former being married to the latter suffered grievously in spiritual matters in consequence.

Amongst the numerous cases of oppression at this time for conscientious resistance to the royal and hierarchical encouragement of "sports," &c. was the well-known one

of Mr. Prynne, a learned Puritan lawyer, who published
a book entitled "The Player's Scourge," severely con-
demning revels, masques, dances, and other sports,
" because he saw the number of plays, play-books, play-
haunters, and play-houses so exceedingly increased, there
being above forty thousand play-books, being now more
vendable than the choicest sermons." For this work
Prynne was fined £50,000, his forehead was branded, his
nose slit, and his ears cut off. Subsequently Dr. Bastwick
and Dr. Burton endured a similar cruel punishment for a
like "offence." Prynne also for a repetition of his faithful
protests was fined an additional £5,000, branded on both
cheeks, the stumps of his ears were further scarred and
burnt, and he and his brother sufferers were then ordered
to be imprisoned for life. Such was a sample of the
Christianity of the "Royal Martyr" and his hierarchy.

It was not, therefore, to be wondered at, that "in 1638
there were eight sail of ships at one time in the river
Thames, bound for New England and filled with Puritan
families; amongst whom were Oliver Cromwell, John
Hampden, and Arthur Haselrigge;" (these ships were,
however, prevented from sailing by an order of the Privy
Council;) or that, "during the twelve years of Laud's
administration, there went over from England about 4,000
Dissenters to settle as planters" in America. (Timpson's
History, p. 340.)

These persecutions continuing year after year, and
threatening ruin and death to the noblest of England's
sons, the sturdy yeomanry of the nation (most of whom
had become Puritans) at length rose as one man, and,
under the leadership of the sincere-hearted Cromwell,

hurled from their seats of power the faithless monarch
with his un-Christian prelates, winning battle after battle
with the sturdy energy which might be expected in truly
pious men, who felt that they were not only fighting for
their civil liberties guaranteed by Magna Charta and the
Petition of Right, but for the house of prayer, the open
Bible, and the very cause of God Himself.

Meanwhile these stirring events, and the general sense
of danger ever present to all thoughtful men, were deve-·
loping some of the noblest lives that have ever adorned
our land. For, as the mountain-pine, when bending in
the roaring wind, thrusts its strong roots still deeper and
more firmly into the abiding rock, so, in these political
storms, the hearts of godly men were constrained to
special trust in the Lord alone, and to such a permanent
closeness of prayerful union with Him that a rare excellence of bold Christian fidelity was the result.

Amid the conflict of contending parties the Scriptures
were increasingly precious to many earnest souls, their
doctrines became the subjects of the deepest interest, and
religious meetings for mutual sympathy and edification
followed as a matter of necessity. But such meetings
were a new thing in English history, and became a source
of bitter hatred and opposition to all concerned in the
long-vested interests of exclusive priesthoods and spiritual
monopolies.

Such meetings (or conventicles, as they were con-
temptuously termed) had indeed commenced during the
reign of Elizabeth, and had necessarily been conducted
with much secrecy and timidity during the sway of King
James and the early portion of that of Charles the

First. But after the downfall of that monarch's ill-used power, the removal of the cruel Laud and Strafford, and the development of popular freedom through the successes of the parliamentary armies, the right of free religious conference in England was first developed in an open and general custom. Precisely at this juncture Quakerism also was developed, and was to a large extent produced by the reaction from the oppressive restraints so long imposed upon religious freedom.

Its founder was one of those contemplative, brooding, but withal boldly resolute characters whom the circumstances of the time were so specially adapted to foster. He inherited the intense feelings and religious enthusiasm of ancestors who had suffered as martyrs for their faith. His mother, Mary Lago, cherished this fervent zeal for godly concerns as the most precious heirloom of her family, and it would appear that to her may be chiefly traced the faith in spiritual realities, and which was a prime feature in her son's character. She was a woman of considerable reading, and of an education beyond that usually enjoyed by persons in her station. This was probably owing to a deep interest in the history of the great religious struggle in which her own relatives had suffered even to the death. She married a husband of congenial disposition—Christopher Fox—a man whose integrity and kindly sympathy for others won for him a local reputation in and around the rural village where he resided, Drayton-in-the-Clay, in Leicestershire, and where he usually went by the name of "Righteous Christer." Like his pious wife he was a zealous attender of the services of the Church of England. His outward circumstances seem to have been more comfortable than his occupation as a weaver might imply, inasmuch as his son George at an early age was supplied with sufficient money to enable him to live, in an economical style, without being necessitated to work for a living; and indeed throughout his career he was free from poverty and straitened circumstances which might otherwise have attended the lot of one whose life was spent in unremunerated itinerant missions, at home and abroad.

George Fox was born in July, 1624, commenced preaching publicly about 1647, was most actively and arduously engaged in mission journeys, and in suffering imprisonments, from 1652 to 1675, and died (aged 66) on the 13th of November, 1690, having been permitted to attain nearly to the "threescore years and ten," and to witness the final security and establishment, by "the Glorious Revolution," of the religious and civil liberties for which he had so valiantly, consistently, and disinterestedly struggled and suffered throughout his life.

His childhood and youth were not eventful, but passed in that deep quietude and seclusion which, even in those stirring times, was a noticeable feature of many parts of the rural districts of England, removed from courts and camps, disturbed neither by mail coaches nor railways, accessible often only by bridle-paths, obtaining news from London at irregular intervals, supplied with wares by pedlars and packhorses, destitute of newspapers, unlighted by gas or oil, and agitated by no public meetings, reform-bills, corn-law leagues, or teetotal societies. But then the summer sunshine in quiet meadows, and the winter evenings in snug-built homely dwellings, fostered in

E

prepared minds a deeper and less interrupted thoughtfulness than the exciting liveliness of these modern days,
when, by means of penny papers, cheap postage, and
universal telegraphic wires, the Land's End and John
o'Groat's House have become, in a manner, mere suburbs
of the bustling Metropolis. Nevertheless, there were
strangely exciting tidings ever and anon conveyed to the
quiet hamlets of those Stuart days; but the intervals for
reflection were long and still. The whirl of the nineteenth
century had not as yet wrung from any distracted poet the
exclamation,—

> "The world is too much with us; late and soon,
>   Getting and spending, we lay waste our powers;
>   Little we see in Nature that is ours."

In the quiet Leicestershire village young George grew
up a silent, pensive, gentle boy,—the darling of his
mother, who watched with more than ordinary maternal
sympathy the development of the deep spiritual consciousness that he had inherited from herself. The boy was in
a certain sense childlike but not childish, docile, obedient,
and most dutiful. He cared little, if at all, for the sports
of the other village lads. It was seen that he was
very observant, especially of the elder folk. He often
startled his parents with grave questions about God and
the things of an immortal existence. The subject of
a future endless life as a simple plain reality seemed,
even in his earliest years, to have taken such a hold of his
mind as oftentimes it is not permitted to, in the most
observant men.

The educational facilities of that age were extremely

limited, there being no national or British schools, very few provincial academies other than a few endowed "grammar schools;" and as Drayton was but a country village there was probably no school whatever in the place. Although thus disadvantageously circumstanced as to education, George learnt to read and write, being taught, most likely, by his excellent mother. This very elementary course was all the instruction he ever received. So that, if in after life his addresses and writings were at times lacking in eloquence, there was no reason to disparage his abilities, which were indeed of a bright and vigorous character. It was very wonderful, considering his scanty education, that he accomplished what he did. Even his literary works fill several thousand closely-printed folio pages.

As George's pensive sober character developed thus early, some of his relatives urged his parents to train him for a clergyman. But it was not so to be. Eventually he was placed with one of those industrious folk, common in country villages, who manage to combine in one business several diverse occupations. George's master was of this description, inasmuch as he was at the same time a wool-dealer, a shoemaker, and a grazier. The wool and sheep department appears to have been that in which George was usually engaged. This was an appropriate occupation for him, from the facilities it afforded for a contemplative out-door life. He engaged in it with much interest, and became a skilful assistant to his master. His quiet, inoffensive disposition, scrupulous honesty and truthfulness, and his deep seriousness, obtained for him general esteem in the neighbourhood. His duties brought him at times to the country fairs; but these were not congenial occasions for the silent, meditative youth. He was not so ascetic as altogether to refuse joining his companions in the quiet ale-house parlours, where the polished oak tables and neatly sanded floors presented a marked contrast to the vile beer-shops and reeking gin-palaces fostered by the unlimited facilities for evil afforded by the lax licensing system of our day ; but when there appeared the slightest tendency to drink more than simple thirst required, George would quietly rebuke his friends, put down his money, and immediately withdraw in sorrow for their misconduct. He was most uncompromising in his own endeavours to maintain a life of inward and outward purity. In his resolute efforts to be faithful and godly he often necessarily appeared unsocial and eccentric to unappreciative observers. In his journal, referring to this period, he quaintly records, "When boys and rude people would laugh at me, I let them alone and went my way ; but people had generally a love to me for my innocency and honesty."

Notwithstanding this goodwill of the neighbours and the deep sympathy of his mother in particular, George felt increasingly solitary, from his inability to find serious friends who could share in his difficulties on various religious questions. In his lonely musings, those heart-searching anxieties which have constituted the early trials of so many eminent Christians, were growing in frequency and force. The gravest doubts and perplexities were taking possession of him.

In this condition of soul, finding no prospect of much spiritual assistance in the remote village, George threw up his wool-dealing and shepherding, and at the age of nineteen betook himself to the neighbouring town of Lutterworth for awhile; but, finding there no effectual relief for his difficulties, he proceeded to other places, taking a room at various towns in succession, as Northampton, Newport Pagnell, and Barnet, and still continuing his meditations and efforts to obtain light and peace. Many a time he paced the silent woodland paths of Barnet Chase, "waiting upon the Lord."

Thence he journeyed on to the great Metropolis, to his uncle Pickering and his Baptist friends. Here he seems to have found more sympathy than anywhere else, and some of the pious people in London wished him to remain with them. This he would perhaps have done had he not received intelligence that his parents and relatives were anxious and grieved at his unsettled state of mind and at his leaving home. He therefore returned to Leicestershire.

Here his friends thought his mind was visionary and excited for want of some engrossing active engagement. It was feared that his quiet life amongst the fields and the long solitary musings in his chamber at night had been a peculiarly unsuitable training for a young man of his taciturn temperament. In order, therefore, to rouse him effectually, his friends urged him to take a wife. On his rejecting this counsel he was advised to enter the army. The parson of the parish, a Mr. Stevens, became much interested in George's case and often visited him. In return, the youth frequently called to converse with the clergyman, and George's thoughtful remarks at their conferences repeatedly furnished matter for the Sunday's sermons in church. Mr. Stevens conceived a high estimate of the young man's piety, and spoke of him to his

parishioners as a worthy example to them. But George
did not feel satisfied with himself, but perseveringly continued his inquiries for spiritual consolation. A neighbouring clergyman recommended him to take tobacco and sing
psalms, thinking he needed soothing influences to counteract his habits of anxious self-examination and cogitation.
George replied, "Tobacco was a thing I did not love, and
psalms I was not in a state to sing." No comfort came
from this source. Another clergyman tried to relieve his
troubles by bleeding him. "But," he records, "they
could not get one drop of blood from me, either in arms
or head (though they endeavoured it); my body being as
it were dried up with sorrow, grief, and troubles, which
were so great upon me that I could have wished I had
never been born, or that I had been born blind, that I
might never have seen wickedness or vanity; and deaf,
that I might never have heard vain and wicked words, or
the Lord's name blasphemed."

Meanwhile he pursued a blameless, kindly life, notwithstanding his deep melancholy. At Christmas time, instead
of joining in the merry-makings, he visited the poor
widows of the parish and gave them alms. When invited
to wedding-parties he declined, but in the course of a few
days he would visit the young couple and give them good
advice. He adds, "and if they were poor I gave them
some money; for I had wherewith both to keep myself
from being chargeable to others and to administer something to the necessities of others." This remark, in
connection with other information respecting his circumstances, indicates a pecuniary condition of considerable
ease, at least for a person in his position.

His religious difficulties still continuing, George Fox withdrew more and more from his clerical and other advisers, relinquished going to church (to the great grief of his relatives) and spent his Sabbaths in reading the Scriptures alone in orchards and fields. When urged by his friends that all believers should go to church, George replied that, "to be a true believer was another thing than they looked upon it to be, and that being bred at Oxford or Cambridge did not qualify or fit a man to be a minister of Christ." He adds, "to neither them, nor any of the Dissenting people could I join with, but was a stranger to all, relying wholly upon the Lord Jesus Christ."

His course of action was not, however, quite consistent with this profession of total religious independence, inasmuch as we presently find him again travelling from place to place, and seeking such persons as took special interest in various theological doctrines. Thus, in one locality he met with a body of persons holding the strange opinion that women have no souls, "no more than a goose;" George's thorough study of the Bible in orchards, fields, hollow oaks, and woodland glades, had furnished him with a remarkable aptitude for the prompt quotation of pertinent texts, and he at once met this doctrine with the words of the blessed Virgin Mary, "*My soul* doth magnify the Lord, and my *spirit* hath rejoiced in God my Saviour." Next, he came amongst a number of visionaries who relied much on dreams. These also he rebuked, and subsequently many of them became his own followers. In this manner, passing from place to place, he wandered through the counties of Derby, Leicester and Nottingham,

still in much distress of mind, often fasting, holding
conference with men of many opinions, but uniting with
none, earnestly striving after peace with God, but not
finding it.

With all his sincere zeal for holiness and his youthful
" innocence," George Fox seems to have not fully appreciated, as yet, the first great principle of God's way of
peace, viz. the entire inability of man either to justify or
sanctify himself, and the consequent necessity for permanent reliance upon a *full free pardon*, as an absolute
and gracious *gift* through the atoning blood of the Lord
Jesus Christ, by whose death on the cross God rendered
it consistent with His perfect crystalline *holiness* to forgive sins even to the *very uttermost*. For inasmuch
as " God was in Christ reconciling the world unto Himself," and inasmuch, also, as " He was wounded *for
our* transgressions" with infinite sufferings, both spiritual
and physical, He has for evermore removed "the enmity."
Hence, with *unlessened irreconcilability to sin*, He " who is
of purer eyes than to behold iniquity," may be approached
with humble penitence by those who have hitherto been the
most impure and sinful of His creatures. To the very
chief of sinners the door of infinite love is thrown open, and
the royal grace of the King of Heaven flows freely to all
who seek it.*

No one can impute the slightest compromise with

* A modern Friend (William Brown, jun., of Shields), in his
work on "Man's Restoration," has, in criticising the defects of
George Fox's theology, very appropriately quoted from a popular
hymn the following instructive stanzas, as illustrating what Fox, in
general, omitted to set forth :—

sin where God *Himself* has *suffered* for sin. That suffering has sent forth Immaculate Holiness to seek for sinners in the lowest depths of their degradation, to elevate them despite of the worst failings, and to transmute, by unmerited gratuitous love, the darkest guilt into permanent purity.

Eventually, after several years of unsatisfactory efforts for rest of soul, George Fox's prayers were graciously

---

> "Let not conscience make you linger,
>   Nor of fitness fondly dream;
> All the fitness He requireth
>   Is to feel your *need* of Him.
> *This He* gives you;
>   'Tis His Spirit's rising beam.
>
> "Come, ye weary, heavy laden,
>   Lost and ruined by the fall!
> If *you tarry till you're better*
>   *You will never come at all.*
> Not the righteous—
>   *Sinners* Jesus came to call."

Christ must be relied on *wholly* for the continuing and future work of sanctification and personal holiness, *as well* as for justification, "the forgiveness of sins that are *past*." William Taylor of California, in his "Infancy and Manhood of Christian Life" (London: S. W. Partridge), shows the root of perpetual failure amongst Christians to arise from their trying to be better disciples by fresh exertions of their own strength, so often proved worthless in the past. He exhorts to daily, total, and renewed recourse to the Lord for strength to live aright, and to confess, "However much I may desire it, and however sincerely I may try, I am sure I can never be any better than I *have* been, nor do better than I have done unless *renewed* in the spirit of my mind."

answered. In the year 1647, at the age of twenty-three, four years after the commencement of his wanderings in search of religious truth, he was enabled to declare:—
"As I had forsaken the priests, so I left the separate teachers also, and those called the most experienced people; for I saw there was none among them all that could speak to my condition. When all my hopes in them and in all men were gone, so that I had nothing outwardly to help me, nor could I tell what to do, then, oh then, I heard a voice which said, 'There is one, even Christ Jesus, that can speak to thy condition;' and when I heard it my heart did leap for joy. Then the Lord let me see why there was none upon the earth that could speak to my condition, namely, that I might give Him all the glory; for all are concluded under sin and shut up in unbelief, as I had been, that Jesus Christ might have the pre-eminence, who enlightens and gives grace and faith, and power. Then the Lord gently led me along and let me see His love which was endless and eternal, surpassing all the knowledge that men have in the natural state, or can get by history or books; and that love let me see myself as I was without Him."

In so far as George Fox thus placed his reliance on Christ only, he found peace and joy. But, nevertheless, he does not appear to have ever arrived at a *full* appreciation of the absolutely *free gift* of God's grace in Christ. He was enabled to lead a life of remarkable faith, prayer and earnest missionary zeal, but it always remained a weak point with him (as for the most part also with his followers till near the middle of the nineteenth century) that he too much omitted to set forth the readiness of the Lord Jesus to receive sinners *just as they are*, and to sanctify them also by successive daily supplies of spiritual strength entirely from Himself, and not from human strivings, other than the strivings of an empty broken heart confessing in fervent prayer its permanent and utter need.

It is perfectly true that on occasion (and especially in the often quoted letter to the Governor of Barbadoes) George Fox acknowledged Christ's work of salvation and an atonement for sins wrought by the one sacrifice on Calvary, but if we regard the *general tenor, the prevailing tone* of his teachings, the full, free, open-handed gratuitous gospel was *not* preached by him or his early followers, in the manner which the general experience of evangelical Christendom has shown to be most successful in bringing peace and conversion to the sinner, or in the precise way by which the Apostlic churches wrought the great work of evangelisation.

Throughout his life, George Fox too much spiritualised away the actuality of the personal manifestation and humanity of the Redeemer. We do not say that he wholly did so (as some of the Hicksites have, more or less, whilst professing to follow Fox's teaching) but he did so to an extent which has at various periods brought grave dangers and trials upon the Society he organised. In connection with this ultra and unscriptural spiritualisation, (or rather, at times, *volatilisation*,) of divine truth, he often virtually, though without intentional disrespect, depreciated the Holy Scriptures. (Some of his immediate followers greatly exceeded him in this error.)

His favourite style of preaching was, " to turn men to the light within," to " Christ *in* them." For he, and

his first followers, held that every man has within him a
"universal and saving light," sufficient in itself to guide
to salvation. He taught that this "light" was the
"primary rule of faith and practice," and that the Holy
Scriptures are *not* the primary rule, inasmuch as the
Divine Spirit who gave forth the Scriptures is superior to
the latter.

A very dangerous fallacy lay concealed at the root of
this doctrine. Doubtless the Divine Author of the Bible
is a higher authority than the latter; but if it has pleased
Him to *ordain* the Scriptures as the chief and universal
source of instruction and guidance for His children, they
are a "primary rule." The guidance of the Holy Spirit
is indeed infallible; but the early Friends continually
ignored the fact that man's *perception* of the Spirit's
guidance is very fallible; generally much more so in fact
than his perception of the meaning of the Scriptures.

Another truth overlooked by the Foxian Quakers was,
that not only a good, but also an evil, spirit sometimes
influences the soul of man, and may readily be mistaken
for right guidance. In so far as inward feelings or
impressions were made a primary test and guidance, a
way was thus opened for the most serious errors.

The Hicksites, a body of American Friends, numbering
about one hundred thousand, and professing a more
enthusiastic reverence for George Fox and his contemporaries than the "orthodox" portion of the Society,
are largely justified in their claims to be the truest representatives of the Foxian Quakers. But they have nevertheless, under the professed guidance of "the inward
light," denied the deity of the Lord Jesus, styled the

Scriptures a "secondary rule" and "a mere written book," rejected the doctrine that salvation is purchased by the personal sufferings of the Saviour, and "spiritualised" away many other of the plain declarations of the Bible.

Probably one of the most thorough and accurate reviews of George Fox's doctrines is that by Samuel M. Janney, of Virginia, U.S., the learned, painstaking, and remarkably impartial author of the American biographies of Penn, Fox, and others. He has carefully collated the eight volumes forming the body of Fox's works. He has shown by collocated passages that the apparent evangelical tone of *some* of Fox's writings (as the letter to the Governor of Barbadoes) was the *exception* rather than *the general* characteristic of his theology.

Janney, in summing up his respective investigations of Fox's works, says "he rejected the doctrine of 'original sin,'"—"he rejected the term Trinity and the idea of tri-personality." "From these and other passages to be cited in the sequel, we cannot avoid the conclusion that George Fox rejected the commonly-received doctrine of satisfaction or vicarious atonement. He did not believe in imputative righteousness." And then at considerable length S. M. Janney shows the grounds which, as he considers, justify the Hicksite section of the Friends in their claims to be the most faithful followers and representatives of Fox and his coadjutors.

Yet George Fox appears to have been virtually more "evangelical" toward the close of his life, than the general scope and purport of his teachings would indicate; but with all his zeal to inculcate genuine sincerity and holiness, he nevertheless continually omitted to enforce some of the fundamental principles of the Gospel. The apology for this grave error must be that a large proportion of the authoritative teachers of "orthodox" religion in those days did not *practically* exemplify or urge the truth that "without holiness no man shall see the Lord," and that as all sin is *abominable* in the Divine sight, there cannot be real acceptance and salvation apart from an *honest abiding repentance.*

Another source of error amongst early Quakerism was the practice (often still observable amongst the Friends) of speaking of the Holy Spirit as *impersonal*, as "the truth," "the inward *principle*," and the "spiritual seed." By also continually speaking of the Lord Jesus as chiefly manifest as "Christ *in* every man," and as identical with this "universal principle," the early Friends lessened the energy and power of the great source of Christian holiness, namely, affection to a living, *personal*, *loving*, suffering Saviour. Men *cannot love* a mere "*principle*," a mere abstract *impersonal* "light."

Hence Quakerism has had its chief secessions through Deistical tendencies. The secessions (in 1827) of the Hicksites, of the Irish Deistical Friends (about the year 1800), and several smaller defections, have been on the side of this heresy. These very secessions have, however, proved that Friends are *not* Deists, but that at the same time there was in the theology of Fox, Barclay, and Penn a dangerous defect, a Deistical *tendency.*[*]

[*] Since writing the preceding paragraph the author has received, through a Friend of Manchester, a printed paper, giving an account of disciplinary proceedings at that meeting (the largest congregation of Friends in Great Britain), intended to repress, in 1868, *renewed*

The characteristic of the Apostolic preaching was not to turn men to internal feelings, to an "inward light," but to Jesus Christ of Nazareth, the Divine Saviour, and to the sacred Scriptures, to which our Lord Himself referred, as " *they* are they which testify of Me." The excessive spiritualisation by Fox and his fellow founders of Quakerism was then carried to perilous lengths. For instance, the term " body and blood of Christ " was constantly explained as if *wholly* spiritual and immaterial.

Thus Penn in his " Christian Quaker" (vol. i. p. 527) : says : " There is no essential difference between the Seed, Light, *Word*, Spirit, Life, Truth, Power, Unction, *Bread*, *Water*, Flesh, *and Blood*, only so denominated from the various manifestations, operations and effects of the *same* Divine *principle in* man." Here we see a likely root of much heresy. A pious and influential Friend, the late John Wilkinson of High Wycombe, who at one period filled the office of presiding clerk (or chairman) of the Friends' Yearly Meeting (a position like that of president of the Wesleyan Conference), and who eventually quitted the Society (in 1836), on account of

---

manifestations of doctrines of an objectionable tendency, and which are calculated to lessen the authority of the Holy Scriptures. These doctrines are being promulgated by several of the most earnest and conscientiously consistent upholders, in that locality, of Barclay's Apology and of the Quaker principles of the Foxian era. They are, however, most distinctly opposed to the principles of evangelical scriptural orthodoxy as generally held by the Churches of Christendom, and by the modern Friends *as a body*, except by the American Hicksites, some of the Philadelphian Friends, and their few English representatives.

what he and others deemed to be its heterodox doctrine, has, in quoting the above words of Penn, made the following just comment: " Compared with this, it would be harmless to lay it down as a principle to begin with in giving children reading lessons, that the letters of the alphabet were all in reality alike, only that they had different shapes." (" Quakerism Examined," p. 167.)

Probably the weakness of early Quakerism on the side of impersonal ideas of Deity has had much to do with its subsequent failure in evangelising the masses. And further, it has been *since* the introduction of more evangelical views into the Society that the Friends have chiefly manifested the philanthropic and missionary zeal which has latterly characterised their sect.

George Fox was a good man; but, being a man, he had his share of fallibility ; and, notwithstanding his undoubted piety, his arduous mission labours, and clear views relative to certain important doctrines, he can by no means be implicitly relied upon on some other points of Christian truth. His chief power and merit consisted in his earnest example of personal piety, his infectious enthusiasm, his judicious ability in selecting and enforcing the doctrines most neglected in his day, and especially in his tact in organising or uniting other godly men for mutual Christian labour.

CHAPTER III.

THE BAPTIST ORIGIN OF QUAKERISM IN GENERAL.

SUMMARY OF FOX'S VIEWS—MOST OF THEM ANTICIPATED BY
THE GENERAL BAPTISTS—PROOFS AND VERIFYING QUOTATIONS
SHOWING THE PREVIOUS BAPTIST ADOPTION OF THE DOCTRINES
AND PRACTICES WHICH ARE OFTEN CONSIDERED TO HAVE
BEEN OF QUAKER OR FOXIAN ORIGIN—THE CHURCH "A
SOCIETY OF EQUALS"—ABROGATION OF CEREMONIES— BELIEF
IN CONTINUANCE OF REVELATION—REJECTION OF INFANT
BAPTISM—BAPTIST OBJECTIONS TO WAR, OATHS, TITHES, ETC.
—THEIR RECOGNITION OF FEMALE USEFULNESS IN THE
CHURCHES—THEIR DISUSE OF NAMES OF MONTHS AND DAYS
DERIVED FROM PAGANISM—BAPTIST DISCIPLINARY RECORDS—
THEIR OVERSIGHT OF MEMBERS—CAUTION RESPECTING THEO-
LOGICAL DEFINITIONS — SOCIAL INTERCOURSE AS A RELI-
GIOUS DUTY—PROTEST AGAINST UNDUE CLAIMS OF HUMAN
LEARNING FOR THE MINISTRY—GRATUITOUS PREACHING OF
MANY EARLY BAPTISTS—PRAISE AND SINGING—FASTING—
MINISTRY OPEN TO ALL MEMBERS — RECOGNITION OF
PREACHERS BY BAPTISTS — MEETINGS FOR DISCIPLINE —
DELINQUENT MEMBERS — MANNER OF MARRIAGE — SYS-
TEMATIC CARE OF THE POOR—BAPTIST USE OF "THEE AND
THOU"—GERMAN MYSTICS ALSO ANTICIPATED FOX'S VIEWS
—HOOKER ON THE EARLY BAPTISTS AND ANABAPTISTS—
SUBSEQUENT DIFFERENCES BETWEEN FRIENDS AND BAPTISTS.

AFTER several years of profound spiritual exercises,
frequent conference with serious persons of various religious opinions (especially amongst the Baptists), and much

F

opportunity for observing the laxity of conduct indulged
in by many nominal "ministers" of the Gospel, George
Fox believed the time was come for zealously extending
his adopted views of Christian truth and ecclesiastical
organisation.

In particular he desired to set forth :—

1. The necessity for a practical individual experience
of God as manifesting a *living*, energizing, and *perceptible*
presence of the Spirit in the souls of men, not merely as a
" God afar off" filling the immensities of the universe, but
also as condescending and willing to reveal His love and
counsels to the lowliest and most humble hearts.

2. The comparative uselessness of studying the Bible
only as a record of past times, dead men, and ancient
experiences, instead of searching it for practical applica-
tions to the every-day life and present wants of each
reader.

3. The duty of " honouring all men," therefore of avoid-
ing undue partiality, flattering titles, or cringing to the
few whilst neglecting the many who were all alike to
be recognised as being God's children, and as having
a glorious immortal life offered to them through Christ.
Hence Christians should seek to elevate and bless all
men, even the repulsive and the debased ; for these latter
should be loved as possessing dormant *capacities* of boundless future development for good.

4. The call and right of *every* Christian to some recognised sphere of usefulness in " the Lord's body,"—the
Church universal, which consists of " many members,"
and has need of the faithful performance of the respective
function of each and every one of them. Hence, spiritual

monopolies were to be guarded against as treason to
the church.

5. The primary importance of aiming at "the essence
and marrow" of all religious matters, rather than resting
in verbal creeds, visible ceremonies, or mere professions.
For our Saviour declared that God seeketh those who are
worshippers of Him "in spirit and in truth."

6. That the ministry of the Gospel, or other spiritual
service, is only to be entered upon under an honest sense
of duty, and to be performed throughout in continual,
humble, prayerful dependence upon the one "Giver of
every good and perfect gift."

These were the main and characteristic principles arrived
at and promulgated by George Fox and his followers.
They were, and are, the essentials of Quakerism.

But these and other kindred principles had, with little
exception, been previously the characteristics of the Baptist
theology also, and more particularly of the "General,"
as distinguished from the "Particular," Baptists. Both
divisions of the Baptists had anticipated most of the
doctrines, and also the system of discipline, adopted by
George Fox and the Friends. But it was the General
Baptists, (who were a distinct body as early as 1608,)
that had most fully arrived at the views and usages which
have been subsequently attributed to Quaker origin.

The differences of opinion which arose amongst the
Baptists (relative to election and reprobation) about the
time of the Civil Wars, resulted in many thousands
joining the ranks of Fox and the Friends. Fox was rather
the *organiser or completing agent*, than the founder of
Quakerism. One special doctrine, that of the "inward

light," was partly original as traceable to him, but even in
this he had been almost wholly anticipated by some of
the German Mystics, as Tauler, and by some English
theologians.

We will now proceed to verify, by quotation and
historic retrospect, the very extensive anticipation of
Quakerism by the early General Baptists and other
Christians.

We find, as a first illustration, that John Smyth, "the
father of the English General Baptists," and a very
intimate friend of the Puritan pastors Robinson and
Ainsworth, who died about A.D. 1610, a generation before
Fox, had earnestly contended for "the beautiful simplicity
of a New Testament church, as a *society of equals*, voluntarily associated, to promote the glory of the Great Head
of the Church."

In 1609, Mr. Smyth published an exposition of the
views held by himself and his associates, and in this
he, like Fox subsequently, bore a strong testimony against
ceremonials in religion, saying, "We affirm that all
the ordinances of the Old Testament—that is, the church,
ministry, worship, and government of the Old Testament
—are abolished; all which were types and shadows of
good things to come, but the body is of Christ."

Like the Friends, too, many of the Puritans and Baptists
believed in the continuance and renewal of inward revelations from God. Thus Neal, in his "History of the
Puritans" (I. 476), states that at the formation of the first
Independent Church, in 1616, "they solemnly covenanted
with each other, in the presence of Almighty God, to walk
together in all God's ways and ordinances, according as He

had already revealed, *or should further make them known*
to them."

Respecting the general influence of the Holy Spirit, one
of the leading Baptists of the seventeenth century—Grantham — in his book on "Primitive Christianity," thus
writes : " Without the influence of God's Spirit, illuminat-
ing our judgments and heightening our affections, and so
evidencing with our spirits that we are the children of
God, we may talk of much, but we truly inherit very little,
of those virtues of which we talk." Another eminent
Baptist of the time—Griffiths—in his "God's Oracle,"
page 30, says: "The Spirit works in us *not only by
its own operations*, but also in an especial manner by the
preaching of the Word."

Smyth and the Baptists rejected infant baptism and the
baptism of ungodly adults. Many of their predecessors—
the Anabaptists—had rejected baptism altogether, in its
outward use. (Fox and the Friends followed the latter in
this respect.) Wickliffe had asserted that children may
be saved without baptism, and that the baptism of water
profiteth not without the baptism of the Spirit. In the
period after Wickliffe many of the Lollards proclaimed
" that Christian people were sufficiently baptised in the
blood of Christ, and needed no water."

(At the commencement of the seventeenth century some
of the Puritans had declared the unscriptural nature of
war, oaths, tithes, and enforced payment for the ministry.)

In 1615, the General Baptists, whilst acknowledging
their allegiance, in temporal matters, to the civil government, vindicated their religious liberty and their responsibility in spirituals to God only, saying, *All men must let*

God alone with His right, who is to be Lord and Lawgiver
of the soul." (Pamphlet entitled " Persecution Judged,"
1615.) For these claims, the Baptists were cruelly persecuted, especially about 1620 (thirty years before the rise
of Quakerism).

It appears, also, that about 1640, it was not uncommon
for women to engage in public discourses, in at least some
of the Baptist congregations, in England (Edwards' " Gan-
græna," part I.) George Fox also sanctioned this custom.

About the year 1643, some of the Baptists, Seekers,
and Independents united in holding meetings in the
Metropolis, to advocate full liberty of conscience, especially as respected the free exercise of the ministry.

Another scruple which was entertained by some of the
Baptists, in common with George Fox and the Friends,
was that respecting the use of the names of the months
and the days derived from pagan or idol times (as
Monday, April, May, &c.)

The entries in the books of discipline of the early
Baptists are almost amusingly identical in form with those
in the corresponding records of the Friends' meetings for
church " business." For instance, the following is the
commencement of the minutes of one of the Baptist
disciplinary meetings in Huntingdonshire :—

" On the seventh day of the Eighth-month, 1655, at a
general meeting of the congregation, held at Papworth
Everard, after prayer and supplication to the Lord, and
some words of doctrine and exhortation, Edmund Mayle
spake as followeth, viz. :

" ' Brethren, according to your order, upon the two-
and-twentieth day of the seventh-month, our brother

Denne and myself went to Wisbeach, where we were joyfully received by the brethren,'" &c. &c.

And so, frequently, if not in general, in the old church-minutes of the Baptists, a similar form of phraseology occurs. We append a few confirmatory instances, viz. :—

The records of the Baptist churches at Spalding, Bourn, and Hackenby, are dated " the 31st day of the 6th month," &c., and contain a list of elders, deacons, and six " gifted brethren," or preachers.

A letter from another Baptist church in Lincolnshire is dated " From Caxton, the 25th day of the 7th month, 1653." Another letter from the same church to the Baptist church at Canterbury, is dated " the 31st day of the 10th month, 1654." It commences thus, " Dear and holy brethren,—Called out from this present evil world, and sanctified through the knowledge of the truth by the Spirit of our God," &c., and concludes with, " Brethren, fare-well. Be of one mind; live in peace," &c. " Your brethren assembled in the name of our Lord Jesus Christ."

The documents issued by the Baptist churches at Ches-ham and Berkhampstead are similarly dated " the 9th day of the 9th month, 1676," &c. The Baptists im-prisoned (for conscience' sake) at Dover, in petitioning the Duke of York for their release, date " the 17th day of the 9th month, 1661." The early records of the Baptists at Biddenden, near Smarden, in Kent, are dated " the twenty-fifth day of the Tenth-month, 1648."

The Baptist system of church discipline resembled in many other particulars that afterwards established by G. Fox, and especially in its care for the poor and over-sight of delinquents.

The Friends have generally been careful to avoid attempts at precise definitions or limitations respecting the nature and personality of the Godhead, and rather to confine themselves to strictly scriptural terms in speaking of so mysterious and awful a subject. Hence, they seldom make use of the terms "Trinity," &c. It appears that, in like manner, the English General Baptists, in the seventeenth century, being "sensible of the grandeur and incomprehensibility of the Deity, and of the weak and limited powers of the human mind, spoke with great caution in their explications of the essence and attributes of the Infinite Being; generally using Scripture terms, and never attempting to explain and define what they reverently deemed, in their own expressive phrase, 'unwordable.'"— (Hist. Gen. Bapt.)

Like the Quakers afterwards, the early Baptists largely cultivated the *social* element and mutual sympathetic intercourse in their religious arrangements. In the 16th Article of the Baptist Conference of A.D. 1611, it was declared that "the members of every church ought to know one another, that so they may perform all the duties of love towards one another, both to soul and body." "*A church ought not to consist of such a multitude as cannot have particular knowledge of one another.*" Hence the Baptist historian observes that "at their first rise the General Baptists did not affect large societies."

Like the Friends, the Baptists employed some of their female members in officially relieving the necessities of the poorer sisters of their denomination. These were called "deaconesses."

Again, like the Friends, the Baptists had, long before

G. Fox's days, from 1610 onwards, protested against the necessity for colleges and learned studies to constitute ministers of the Gospel. They admitted the value of learning as a subsidiary, but not as an essential, and urged four reasons, viz.—" 1. The Gospel was at first preached and brought forth into the world by unlearned men; such were the apostles. 2. Amongst the many qualifications required in the Scriptures, to be found in those that are set apart to the work and office of an elder, we never find this recorded as one. 3. Experience testifies that men unlearned in the languages have been very useful in the Lord's hand, and famous instruments for the good of souls. 4. In all ages learned men have introduced and defended the errors of Popery and persecuted the true Christians."

It is further stated in the "History of the Baptists," (I. 420,) that, in the seventeenth century, "most of their ministers carried on business"; and it is evident from *their earliest records*, that they seldom received anything from the congregation, except travelling expenses, &c. And when the increase of the cause and other circumstances rendered it necessary to contribute to their support, it was in many places yielded to with great reluctance. So late as 1679 it was considered, at Berkhampstead, as a crime worthy of church censure to affirm "that men ought to have a set maintenance by the year for preaching."

Mr. Francis Stanley, an active and godly Baptist minister in the time of the Commonwealth, declared his knowledge that "some ministers had spent a great part of their outward substance in the service of the churches; some their all, and some more than their all; many being reduced to the affecting strait, either to neglect the worthy work of the Gospel, or else to be reported worse than infidels, 1 Tim. v. 8." Here, again, we see a prominent Quaker "testimony" anticipated and carried out by the Baptists.

Respecting praise and singing, Mr. Grantham, a prominent minister of the early Baptists, wrote that "such persons as God hath gifted to tell forth His mighty acts, and to recount His special providence, and upon whose hearts God hath put a lively sense of present mercies, should have their liberty and convenient opportunity to celebrate the high praises of God, *one by one*, in the churches of God; and that, with such words *as the nature of the matter and present occasion require.*"

As to oaths, the early Baptists' declaration of faith stated: " We further declare that, as we are to be a peaceable people upon the account of action, so we look upon it to be our duty to keep ourselves from oaths, engagements, and covenants, either for or against this or that person, government, or persons whatsoever. ' For because of swearing the land mourneth.' Jer. xxiii. 10." —Crosby's Hist. Baptists.

In his Journal, George Fox repeatedly mentions his practice of fasting. On one occasion he appears to have fasted for ten days. The Baptists had also attached some importance to this exercise. These generally fasted from six in the morning till six in the evening, spending the interval in reading the Scriptures, solemn prayer, and exhortation, accompanied with acts of charity. For example, we find the Baptist church at Amersham holding a united fast on account of the trials and difficulties of their congregation, and recorded subsequently in their book of minutes the following entry : " The ninth of the eighth-month, the church kept as a day of thanksgiving to Almighty God, because He had been pleased to give most of the things which we had been seeking to Him for by fasting and prayer." In Pepys's Diary (May 8, 1656) he writes, at Ipswich, " I had the curiosity to visit some Quakers here in prison ; a new fanatic sect of dangerous principles, who show no respect to any man, magistrate or other,* and seem a melancholy proud sort of people, and exceedingly ignorant. One of these was said to have fasted twenty days, but another endeavouring to do the like perished on the tenth, when he would have eaten but could not." .

The Quaker plan of recognising and· encouraging the gifts of the individual members of the churches was in general exercise by other sects during the Civil Wars before the rise of Quakerism, and afterwards in the time of Cromwell's administration. Many instances and illustrations of this occur in the histories of the period, also in the general literature of the time—whether Hudibrastic or grave. For example, the General Baptists at Spalding held a prayer meeting every Wednesday, " that our brethren, as many of them as can, lay out themselves in such a manner for the Lord as seems most to answer the gifts given them of the Lord, that so a discovery may be made of that precious treasure of preaching and

---

* The Quakers, on the contrary, were taught to "honour all men," and it especially annoyed the magistrates and clergy that the new sect often treated the poor and lowly with as much respect as themselves.

expounding the Word which, it is hoped, may tend to the
glorifying of our Heavenly Father and the edifying of
one another."

Others, besides the Baptists, especially the Independents,
taught the diffusion of spiritual gifts throughout the
members of the churches. Thus, William Dell—who held
the living of Yeldon, and was afterwards Master of Caius
College, Cambridge—published in 1645 a work entitled,
" Power from on High ; or, the Power of the Holy Ghost
dispersed through the whole body of Christ and communicated to each Member."

When any one of the Baptist brethren had exercised
his gifts for a considerable time with acceptance to the
congregation, such a one was recorded as " a brother confirmed in the ministry." In most churches there were
several such recorded ministers. The Friends have
adopted the same plan, using also the term " recorded
minister," or " acknowledged minister."

The Baptists and the Friends in the seventeenth
century alike termed their gatherings for church government " meetings for discipline." In these disciplinary
assemblies the Baptists " considered Christ as the sole
Governor of his Church, and the precepts of the New
Testament as the only rules of discipline." Their historian says : " All their records which have fallen under our
notice afford pleasing evidence of this, *for scarcely any
decision of moment is entered without a reference to the
texts of Scripture on which it is founded.*" In this scriptural simplicity the Baptist discipline *surpassed* that of
the Friends, who have gradually accumulated a compen-
dious code of discipline—forming a printed volume of 240

pages—which is sometimes administered with more formality and reverence for sectarian traditions than simple reference to the authority of Scripture.

The Baptists held their "meetings for discipline" monthly, quarterly, and yearly. So do the Friends. They appointed some of their members to watch over the others for their good. These were styled "helps in government." The Friends have similar officers, who are named "overseers."

The early Baptists attached considerable importance to the avoidance of "superfluity of apparel." So have the Friends, though often mistaking formalistic peculiarity for simplicity. In 1628 the Kentish Baptists recorded the following resolution:—"Agreed that the soul-condemning sin of pride be utterly extirpated and rooted out from amongst us, and that all the discriminating characters thereof, to wit, superfluity of apparel, &c. be utterly extinguished."

. At the Quarterly Meetings of the General Baptists regular inquiries were instituted into the character and conduct of the members. The same plan was subsequently adopted by the Friends, who have framed ten "queries," which are read and answered in writing at least once a year, and oftener as to some of the inquiries. Summaries of these answers form the subject of collective deliberation at the annual meeting. The doctrines preached by the ministers formed a regular subject of church inquiry, as also the regular attendance of meetings for worship by each member.

Delinquent Baptist members were at first dealt with by private remonstrance; this failing, the "meetings for

discipline " took them in hand. If still obdurate, the
offenders were, after three admonitions, excluded. The
Quaker plan is almost identical. The latter do not, however, require—as the Baptists did—that persons laying a
complaint against the conduct of a member shall certify
the same with their signatures in a letter to the over-
seeing officers of the church.

At the Baptist meetings for discipline there were sometimes appeals issued for assistance to other similar
meetings — as amongst the Friends. For example,
we find the Baptist meeting at Warboys thus writing
to a neighbouring congregation : " Brethren,—Forasmuch as many differences have happened between
William Dunn and Thomas Chapman, elders of the
church at Warboys, we beseech you to send one or two of
your elders to hear the said differences—and so help the
brethren at Warboys with your advice for ending of them."

The Baptists surpassed the Friends in mercy to
expelled members, inasmuch as the former sent repeated
invitations to such persons, imploring them by special
messengers to repent of past evil deeds, and offering a
welcome back on sincere compliance. These messages
were often continued at intervals till the death of the
expelled. The Friends, with some exceptions, have taken
little further care of their excommunicated members.

The Baptists also anticipated the Friends in their
thorough care of the poorer members of the church. Their
relief to the latter was very liberal. We find, that in 1652
some of their followers made it a trade to go from place
to place to seek relief from the churches.

The Friends' mode of solemnising marriages is almost

identical with that previously established by the early Baptists. Both sects required preliminary notice to be given to the church, in time to allow proper inquiries as to parental approval, &c. After a mutual promise of fidelity and affection "till the Lord by death shall separate us," the pair "took each other" in marriage, and then signed a "certificate" to that effect. The congregation present also signed the same, after which it was carefully registered and preserved. The Quaker custom is nearly the same.

Like the Friends, the Baptists were much troubled by their members "marrying out" of the church. Both denominations in general "disowned" the delinquents. But, till recently, the Friends were more harsh in such cases than the Baptists, for the latter usually only discharged the offenders temporarily; but the Friends have often promptly and permanently dismissed such—by scores per annum—and thereafter treated them as if grave moral delinquents. During the past ten years a wiser and more merciful principle has regulated this branch of the Quaker discipline.

Many of the early Baptists used the singular pronouns "thou" and "thee" in addressing individuals. This custom the Quakers have, as a body, adopted till very recently. It is now falling into disuse.

Altogether, the resemblance, or often the identity, of the Quaker institutes with those of the Baptists is so complete, that the Society of Friends may truly be termed an offspring of the Baptist denomination. George Fox appears to have long and carefully studied the doctrine and discipline of that godly people, and to have largely gathered the constitution of Quakerism from this source. But it is extraordinary that so very little, if any, acknowledgment of the same has been made by himself, or by his successors, hitherto.

One of the reasons why the General Baptists received less attention during the latter half of the seventeenth century —the era of the establishment of Quakerism—was from the circumstance that their meetings were often, if not usually, held in private houses. (Taylor's History, page 317.) Yet the sect was widely distributed over England, especially in the midland and eastern counties, and in London.

In 1615 the General Baptists published a protest against the numerous persecutions of their members for conscience' sake. They complain that "many of them were exposed to want, lost their estates, and were confined in noisome dungeons till death released them." Many years later they complain bitterly of "persecuting priests" who "hale us before the judgment seats." In Charles the Second's reign many hundreds of them were imprisoned.

The Baptist histories often mention their members as joining the Friends' Society. Thus, at Littleport, near Ely, twelve out of thirty-four members became Friends. "Many " of the Baptists of Fenstanton and Yelling are mentioned as becoming Quakers. Similar defections are recorded in Essex, Kent, &c.

Fox went *beyond* the Baptists in rejecting *all* outward baptism and the outward celebration of the Lord's Supper. Doubtless the Baptists would say that he here went beyond Scripture also. But here again the Lollards had anticipated him.

In the " History of the English (Particular) Baptists,"
by Thomas Crosby (five vols), London, 1738, there are
to be found many further illustrations of the similarity of
the early doctrine and discipline of the Baptist Church to
that of the Friends; but not so strikingly shown as in
the histories and records of the General Baptists.

The practice of silent waiting upon God, so characteristic of the Friends, had long ago been cherished by
the German and other " Mystics." These excellent men,
as Tauler, Jacob Behmen and others, were Quakers
before Fox. T. Hancock, author of " The Peculium,"
(prize essay) says (p. 149) : " I do not think it has ever
been noticed that Giles Calvert the publisher of all the
first Quaker tracts, was also publisher of the English
translation of Behmen. Some early passages of Fox's
journal are singularly Behmenistic." He elsewhere remarks : " The Quaker prohibitions of music, of mourning
habits, of gravestones, and almost every other item of the
' Book of Discipline,' arose from the Puritan spirit of
the seventeenth century contributed to Quakerism."

There is now lying before the writer an old folio copy
of Hooker's " Ecclesiastical Polity," printed by R.
Bishop, London, 1638 (ten years before the rise of
Quakerism). In the introductory remarks is a striking
passage, where the author, describing the Baptists and
their Anabaptist predecessors (some of whom were
Lollards and Wickliffites in the preceding centuries),
shows conclusively their anticipation of some of those which
have often been represented as " peculiar testimonies " of
Quakerism. Hooker says :

" Amongst others there sprang up presently one kind

o

of men, with whose zeal and forwardness, the rest being
compared, were thought to be marvellous cold and dull.
They secretly made their doleful complaint everywhere as
they went, that albeit the world did begin to profess some
dislike of that which was evil in the kingdom of darkness,
yet fruits worthy of a true repentance were not seen ; and
that if men did repent as they ought, they must endeavour
to purge the truth of all manner of evil. Private repentance, they said, must appear by every man's fashioning
his own life contrary unto the custom and orders of this
present world both in greater things and in less. To this
purpose they had always in their mouths those greater
things—charity, faith, the true fear of God, the cross, the
mortification of the flesh.

"They were solicitors of men to fast, to often meditations of heavenly things ; and, as it were, conferences
in secret with God, by prayers not framed according to
the frozen manner of the world, but expressing such
fervent desires as might even force God to hearken
unto them.

" Where they found men in diet, attire, furniture of
house, or any other way observers of civility and decent
order, such they reproved as being carnally and earthly
minded. Every word otherwise than severely and sadly
uttered seemed to pierce like a sword through them. If
any man were pleasant, their manner was presently with
sighs to repeat those words of our Saviour Christ, ' Woe
be to you which now laugh, for ye shall lament.' So
great was their delight to be always in trouble that such
as did quietly lead their lives, they judged of all other
men to be in most dangerous case.

" They so much affected to cross the ordinary custom
in everything, that when other men's use was to put on
better attire, they would be sure to show themselves
openly abroad in worse. The ordinary names of the days
in the week, they thought it a kind of profaneness to use,
and therefore accustomed themselves to make no other
distinction than by numbers, ' the first,' ' second,' ' third
day.'

" From this they proceeded to public reformation, first
ecclesiastical and then civil. Touching the former, they
boldly avouched that themselves only had the truth, which
thing upon peril of their lives they would at all times
defend, and that, since the Apostles lived, the same was
never before in all points sincerely taught.

" Wherefore, that things might again be brought to
that ancient integrity which Jesus Christ, by his word
requireth, they began to control the ministers of the
Gospel for attributing so much force and virtue unto the
scriptures of God read; whereas the truth was that when
the Word is said to engender faith in the heart and to
convert the soul of man, or to work any such spiritual
divine effect, these speeches are not thereunto applicable,
as it is read or preached, but as it is engrafted in us by
the power of the Holy Ghost, opening the eyes of our
understanding, and so revealing the mysteries of God,
according to that which Jeremiah promised before
should be, saying : ' I will put my law in their inward
parts, and I will write it in their hearts.' "

Hooker continues this description at great length,
alluding further to their " forbidding oaths, the necessary
means of judicial trial, because Christ hath said ' Swear

not at all.' " He somewhat severely writes, "when they and
their Bibles were alone together, what strange fantastical
opinion at any time entered into their heads, their use was
to think the Spirit taught it them. And forasmuch as
they were of the same suit with those of whom the
Apostle speaketh, saying, 'they are still learning but
never attain to the knowledge of truth,' it was no marvel
to see them every day broach some new thing not heard of
before, which restless levity they did interpret to be their
going on to spiritual perfection and a proceeding from
faith to faith."

Further on, Hooker speaks of " their wonderful show
of zeal toward God, wherewith they seemed to be even
rapt in everthing they spake," and " the bountiful relief
wherewith they eased the broken estate of such needy
creatures as were in that respect the more apt to be
drawn away."

This remarkable portrait of the Anabaptists (mainly
based on a similar one in a French writer, Guy de Bres),
if written some sixty years later, might have been styled
in general, a portrait of Quakerism. The resemblance is
in many respects (allowing for some prejudices) minutely
exact. The inference is plain—Quakerism was mainly a
copy and continuation of the Anabaptist and Baptist
system. (Hooker died November 2, 1600—*fifty years
before the rise of Quakerism.*)

And no Friend need be ashamed of tracing his spiritual ancestry to Baptists and Anabaptists. (The two
were in general identical, but the latter was the name
mostly given prior to about 1600.) The contempt with
which advocates of spiritual monopolies have sought to

invest all Anabaptists on account of the extravagances of
a few professors of their views in one locality (Munster
in Germany), is most undeserved. Even those Munster
men were rebels against the cruelty of German tyrants,
whose oppressions over the souls and bodies of the com-
monalty, then actual serfs and bondsmen, were often,
without exaggeration, diabolical. They failed and were
rebels. Had they conquered, men would have styled
them heroes and patriots. Their rebellion was ferocious, because their oppressors had been far more
ferocious.

But these few Anabaptists of Munster were not by any
means examples of the generality of Anabaptists or
Baptists. As a whole these Christians were (and their
representatives still are, in the nineteenth century),
eminent for the best virtues of godliness and scriptural obedience. And their Quaker offspring have followed them in the good example, thus received as an
inheritance.

About a quarter of a century after the rise of Quakerism some disputes sprang up between the Friends and the
(Particular) Baptists. Several public discussions were
held in London, in which it appears that, according to
the general impression of the public, the Friends had the
worst of the argument. The Quaker Thomas Ellwood
(Milton's friend) alludes somewhat cheerfully to the result
of a provincial discussion with Baptists at Wycombe, in
a Latin couplet—

> " Prævaluit veritas; inimici terga dedére:
> Nos sumus in tuto; laus tribuenda Deo."

This he thus translates—

> " Truth hath prevailed; the enemies did fly;
> We are in safety; praise to God on high."

However, the Baptist account might perhaps indicate a different result.

Many years later, in 1717, some weak brethren of each sect desired to "discuss" publicly with each other; whereupon the more judicious men of both denominations wrote a letter exhorting all parties to quietness and peace. This letter was signed by five leading Baptists and as many principal Friends, including the venerable George Whitehead (then aged eighty-one), the last survivor of the first establishers of Quakerism. (He had begun to preach in 1655 at the age of nineteen; in his declining years he was regarded as the Nestor of the Quakers; he died, aged eighty-seven, in 1723.)

This letter of advice wisely exhorted the disputants "not to insist upon such public ways of striving with each other, seeing there are other methods which will be less offensive, and more informing, to them who are in search of truth." (Crosby's Hist. Bapt.)

George Fox says of many of the doctrines and customs long previously adopted by the Baptists and Puritans, that he was "moved" to declare them. "It was opened to me" is another of his favourite phrases. But it is plain, from the preceding and many other historic proofs, that his "movings" and "openings" were not new information, except through the instrumentality and medium of other men and their interpretations of Scripture.

Fox's "openings" were in fact his terms for spiritual

acquiescence with, and *approval of,* such and such doctrines or usages. He explains his own meaning of this in a passage where he records in his Journal (I. 92), " For though I read the Scriptures that spoke of Christ and of God, yet I knew Him not *but by revelation,* as He who hath the key did open, and as the Father of life drew me to his Son by his Spirit." It is of course utterly preposterous to conclude from this that the facts of Scripture were afresh " revealed " independently to Fox. But his own language is awkwardly ambiguous.

The question will doubtless occur to many,—Seeing, then, that the early Friends and the early Baptists were at first so nearly identical in doctrine and discipline, whence is it that the subsequent influence of the former has, in proportion to their numbers, been so much greater than that of the latter ?

To this it may be replied, that the Friends have far more thoroughly *acted out* and persistently *maintained* the original Baptist principles and *discipline.* They have been much more *conservative* of their early principles and constitution.

The General Baptists have not continued as they were. Their discipline has, in particular, been greatly relaxed. The Friends are their modern *representatives,* even more than the present Baptist churches. The General Baptists may almost be said to have *gone over in a body to the Friends, in many districts ;* at any rate they no longer exist separately in their Quaker-like form of the seventeenth century. In other words, a gradual revolution has changed much of the *distinctive* element of the early Baptists. Charles H. Spurgeon is perhaps their nearest

modern representative *as a Baptist*, and hence, as is well
known, he has large unity with the Friends. Hence also
much of his special success as a Christian minister.

Further, the doctrine of individual religious responsibility was carried out much further by Fox than by the
General Baptists. He far more absolutely referred his
hearers to the sufficiency of *individual* personal access to
God for *all* religious and moral purposes. He also more
fully and repeatedly recognised the perceptibility and the
individualising visitations of the Spirit of God. Hence
the Friends have attained an unequalled activity by their
freedom from mediate and ministerial control in religious
matters, whilst still retaining reverence and fidelity to
their one Lord by individual independent access.

The generality of other sects (the modern Baptists
included), with all their excellencies, do not so fully leave
their members *alone with God*. They interpose more of
the authority or special influence of spiritual chiefs and
pastors, instead of the more direct theocratic rule of the
republic of Friends.

CHAPTER IV.

FOX'S FIRST MINISTRY IN THE MIDLANDS AND IN YORKSHIRE.

COMMENCEMENT OF FOX'S MINISTRY — SILENT WORSHIP — CONFLICTS IN THE VALE OF BELVOIR—DIVINITY, PHYSIC, AND LAW—FIRST IMPRISONMENT—VIOLENTLY ASSAULTED AT MANSFIELD—AGAIN IMPRISONED AT DERBY—LICHFIELD ADVENTURE — ON CHRISTIAN PERFECTION — UNDERGOES GREAT OPPOSITION IN YORKSHIRE—THE CHURCH "MILITANT" AT YORK, WAKEFIELD, DONCASTER, ETC.—THE MAN IN LEATHER BREECHES — FAVOURED BY THE SOLDIERY — CROMWELL — PHYSICAL ASPECTS OF ENGLAND IN THE SEVENTEENTH CENTURY—THE CLERGY AND THE YEOMANRY.

THERE is a remarkable contrast observable between the ripened Christian judgment manifested by George Fox in the middle and concluding stages of his life, as compared with the rashness sometimes exhibited during his first years of public action. By the fervours of young and inexperienced zeal he was then involved in much trouble.

His discourses were mainly of two kinds ; first, those for the edification and comfort of awakened persons ; secondly, those for the denunciation of evil-doers and of presumed sources of error. The latter class of addresses was often of questionable effect as to any good, and was certainly productive of sturdy opposition and bitter passion. It is instructive to observe how, in the New

Testament, the denunciatory passages, even of inspired writers, are few and far between. The Gospel is, as its name implies, good tidings of great joy—the invitations of the united love and holiness of God in Christ. If this principle had been more fully recognised by the early Friends much greater success might have attended their labours, and with far less strife and pain. Yet the preaching of the cross will always be "an offence" or "foolishness" to a certain class of hearers.

George Fox's public ministry commenced about 1647, and was chiefly addressed, at first, to companies of serious persons scattered through parts of Leicestershire, Warwick, Derby, and Nottingham. The quiet pastoral regions of the Trent valley and the Derbyshire hills were the cradle of Quakerism. In these districts the Baptists were specially the objects of Fox's visits. Thus, on coming into Nottinghamshire at this period, he writes : " I found there a company of shattered Baptists and others ; and the Lord's power wrought mightily and gathered many of them." (Journal, I. 104.) In Leicestershire also he says, at this time, " There were some Baptists in that county whom I desired to see and speak with." In other parts of England, subsequently, the Baptists, at least the " General" Baptists, united themselves to Fox " in shoals."

The chief matter urged upon these companies of pious persons was the importance of cultivating inward watchful communion with the Spirit of the Lord. This eminently edifying exercise was generally styled by George Fox "waiting" upon God. " The Mystics," a very interesting, much misrepresented, but undoubtedly holy, class of persons, have usually styled it "recollectedness of spirit." Some of the Moravians also cherish the same exercise, but with more direct reference to the contemplation of the presence (at God's right hand in heaven) of the glorified *Person* of the Lord Jesus.

As George Fox's auditors increased in the cultivation of this habit, especially in their collective gatherings, their assemblies became characterised by a remarkable solemnity which powerfully affected many beholders, often gained further adherents, and exercised a powerful and permanent effect on the life and conversation of those who practised these earnest prayerful introspections and retro-spections. A description of Fox and the Quaker meetings at this early period is thus given by Thomas Thompson, one of the first Friends gathered in Yorkshire:

"In the fore part of the year 1652 it pleased the Lord to order His faithful and valiant servant and messenger, dear George Fox, into these parts; but I had not then opportunity to see him, though I greatly desired it. But some of my familiars that were with him, gave me an account of his manner of life, and also of his doctrine; they told me that he was in his behaviour very reserved, not using any needless words or discourses that tended not to edification, and thus he used not respect of persons, very temperate in his eating and drinking, his apparel homely yet decent; as for his doctrine he directed people to the light of *Christ in their consciences*, to guide them to God.

"Now it happened that about the sixth or seventh month of the year 1652, we heard of a people raised up at or about Malton that were called Quakers; which was

the first time that I heard of that name being given to
any people. They were by most persons spoken against;
but when I strictly enquired what any had to lay to their
charge, that might give cause for such aspersions as were
thrown upon them, I met with none who could justly
accuse them of any crime; only they said they were a
fantastical and conceited people, and burnt their lace and
ribbons and other superfluous things which formerly they
used to wear, and that they fell into strange fits of
quaking and trembling." On the arrival of the Friends
near Bridlington, with William Dewsbury (a companion
of George Fox), T. T. went to see them. He adds:
"Coming into the room where William was, I found him
writing, and the rest of his company were sitting in great
silence, seeming to be much retired in mind and fixed
towards God; their countenances, grave and solid withal,
preached unto me and confirmed what I had before believed, that they were the people of the Lord. After a
little time William ceased writing, and many of the
town's-people coming in, he began, in the power and
wisdom of God, to declare the truth. And oh, how was
my soul refreshed; and the witness of God reached in
my heart; I cannot express it with pen. I had never
heard nor felt the like before, for he spake as one having
authority and not as the scribes; so that if all the world
said nay I could have given my testimony that it was the
everlasting truth of God.

"And in the same month my mouth was livingly
opened to declare the name of the Lord and preach
repentance to the people: and the work of the Lord
prospered in the hands of His faithful servants; and I

knew a bridle to my tongue, and was greatly afraid lest I should offend Him in thought, word, or deed."

Whilst comforting and instructing many companies of such pious persons in the Midlands, George Fox at times had returns of his former inward conflicts. Thus, whilst preaching in the Vale of Belvoir, he records: "One morning, as I was sitting by the fire, a great cloud came over me, and a temptation beset me; but I sat still. And it was said, "All things come by nature." But as I sat still and said nothing, the people of the house perceived nothing. And as I sat still under it and let it alone, a living hope arose in me and a true voice, which said, 'There *is* a living God, who made all things.' And immediately the cloud and temptation vanished away—and I praised the living God. After some time I met with some people who had a notion that there was no God, but that all things came by nature. I had a great dispute with them, and overturned them, and made some of them confess that there is a living God. Then I saw that it was good that I had gone through that exercise."

Fox's indignation was greatly excited against the exclusiveness of the clergy, and especially against making a mere profession of preaching, and against undue reverence for churches. Inasmuch as the term a "Church" is in the Bible applied to any congregation of believers, Fox refused to use it in speaking of a building, holding also that episcopal consecration was a delusion. Hence he and his companions usually styled the Church edifices "steeple-houses."

George says, "The Lord opened to me three things,

relating to those three great professions in the world,
physic, divinity (so called) and law. He showed me that
the physicians were out of the wisdom of God; that the
priests were out of the true faith, which Christ is the
author of, the faith which purifies and gives victory; also
that the lawyers were out of the equity, and out of the
true justice and out of the law of God."

"But the black earthly spirit of the priests wounded
my life; and when I heard the bell toll to call people
together to the steeple-house, it struck at my life; for it
was just like a market-bell to gather people together,
that the priest might set forth his wares to sale. Oh!
the vast sums of money that are gotten by the trade they
make of selling the scriptures, and by their preaching, from
the highest bishop to the lowest priest! What one trade
else in the world is comparable to it?" (Journal I. 117.)

With these feelings, George came one day in 1649, to
Nottingham, and there his attention was attracted to a
large church on the hill, of which he writes: "The Lord
said unto me, 'Thou must go and cry against yonder great
idol, and against the worshippers therein.' When I came
there, all the people looked like fallow-ground, and the
priest (like a great lump of earth) stood in his pulpit
above." Here George interrupted the minister whilst
preaching, and, it must be acknowledged, very inap-
propriately. It was not to be wondered at that he
was speedily stopped. He adds, "As I spoke thus
amongst them, the officers came and took me away
and put me into a nasty stinking prison, the smell
whereof got so into my nose and throat, that it very much
annoyed me."

After an imprisonment of "a pretty long time" in Nottingham Gaol, George was liberated, and proceeded to Mansfield Woodhouse. Unintimidated by his recent confinement he writes, "I was moved to go into the steeple-house there and declare the truth to the priest and people; but the people fell upon me in great rage, struck me down, and almost stifled and smothered me ; and I was cruelly beaten and bruised by them with their hands, bibles and sticks. Then they haled me out, though I was hardly able to stand, and put me into the stocks, where I sat some hours; and they brought dog-whips and horse-whips, threatening to whip me." Eventually these cowardly savages stoned their visitor out of the town.

In other places he was received with kindness, and many persons embraced his views, and took to the habit of worshipping in the silent, contemplative, "waiting" reverence of soul which he recommended. At Coventry he heard of some fanatics confined in the gaol there, who denied the existence of God. He says, "As I walked towards the gaol the word of the Lord came to me, saying, 'My love was always to thee, and thou art in My love.' And I was ravished with the sense of the love of God, and greatly strengthened in my inward man." Arrived at the prison, he found in it a wild group of "Ranters" who professed to be God. George, with his usual shrewd repartee, promptly confounded them by a few such questions as "Whether it will rain to-morrow?" &c.

Continuing his itinerant ministry he came to Derby, and going into the church, waited till the service was ended, when he began to address the people there. This was a custom often permitted in those days, provided it

were done with order and courtesy. However, George was
arrested and eventually imprisoned for blasphemy. This
charge was based upon his declarations that he was "in
the paradise of God;" and on being asked if he had no
sin, he replied, "Christ, my Saviour, has taken away my
sin, and in Him there is no sin."

As we have already remarked, Fox was throughout his
life a man of a truly reverend and godly spirit; but in his
early career, and amid the excitements of the times and of
the novelty of his own position, he often laid himself open
to serious misunderstandings by some of his expressions,
and by the positive assertion of his individual feelings as
the communications of the Lord's Spirit. This was a
common error with many persons in that and the preceding age. Concerning such, the judicious Hooker
pertinently writes: "Most sure it is that when men's
affections do frame their opinions, they are, in defence of
error, more earnest a great deal than—for the most part
—sound believers in the maintenance of *truth apprehended
according to the nature of that evidence which Scripture
yieldeth*. It is not, therefore, the fervent earnestness of
their persuasions, but the *soundness of those reasons* whereupon the same is built, which must declare their opinions
in these things to have been wrought by the Holy Ghost,
and not by the fraud of that evil spirit which, even in his
illusions, is strong."

Some of George Fox's early utterances were certainly
lacking in the common sense which in general characterised him. Thus, at one time he declares, "Now was I
come up in spirit through the flaming sword into the
paradise of God. All things were new. I knew nothing

but pureness, and innocency and righteousness, being renewed up into the image of God by Jesus Christ; so that I say 1 was come up to the state of Adam which he was in before he fell." Again, " In the year 1648, I saw there was a great crack to go throughout the earth, and a great smoke to go as the crack went; and that after the crack there should be a great shaking ; this was the earth in people's hearts which was to be shaken," &c. On another occasion, seeing at a distance the three spires of Lichfield, he records, " They struck at my life. I stepped away and went by my eye over hedge and ditch till I came within a mile of Lichfield." Here, although it was winter, he took off his shoes, being so " commanded by the Lord," and proceeding barefoot into the city, went up and down the street crying out, " Woe to the bloody city of Lichfield ! " Having discharged this apprehended duty, he did what most reasonable men would have done beforehand, viz. he began to consider " why, or for what reason, I should be sent to cry against that city, and call it the bloody city." " Afterwards I came to understand, that in the Emperor Diocletian's time a thousand Christians were martyred in Lichfield." With this very vague and questionable "reason" George appears to have satisfied himself.

A few harmless escapades and rhapsodies, such as the preceding, have led to Fox being styled a fanatic and a ranter by his enemies. But these were exceptional occurrences. The main tenour of his life, especially in later years, was characterised by wonderful prudence and Christian wisdom. Some of his friends have injured his character, by refusing to concede the error of some of his

H

early weaknesses. As to his professions of "innocence" and
being "without sin," we may remember that, in a certain
sense, the New Testament recognises perfection as an
attainable duty in this life. Peter exhorts : " Be diligent
that ye may be found of Him in peace, without spot, and
blameless." (2 Pet. iii. 14.) Paul prays for the Thessa-
lonians, "The very God of peace sanctify you wholly,"
(1 Thess. v. 23,) and exhorts the Romans : " Present
your bodies a living sacrifice, holy, acceptable unto God.
(Rom. xii. 1.)

But George Fox and the early Friends sometimes spoke
ambiguously of " perfection," and hence gave offence even
to good men. They did not with sufficient clearness
represent this requirement to be a thoroughly repentant
trust for the gift of justification or perfect pardon for past
sins, through the propitiation of the Lord Jesus, and continual prayerful dependence on the same Lord Jesus for
perfect sanctification also, or for the whole supply of the
present and future daily recurring need for strength to
continue in His way.

Of this condition William Taylor, the Californian
Methodist "revivalist," says : "The very nature of the
work shows its adaptation to this life. The idea of a
soldier never becoming loyal till he is dying ; or of a wife
remaining infidel to her husband till she is closing her
eyes in death ! The idea that we can't be holy till we
come to die is ridiculous. The heart may be full of love
to-day, but will expand and contain more to-morrow.
Christian perfection, instead of fixing a limit to Christian
attainment, is the grand preliminary basis for a rapid,
felicitous, growing up into Christ, that will certainly go

on to the close of our mortal struggle, and will probably be *as illimitable* as eternity."—"Infancy and Manhood of Christian Life." London: S. W. Partridge.

But George Fox's plea of perfection at Derby was deemed heretical and dangerous; and for this and other statements he was detained a year in prison there. George manifested so much patience, goodwill, and cheerfulness in his confinement, that he gained many friends amongst those who visited him. The jailor treated him with great kindness, and permitted him privileges not accorded to the other prisoners. George's relatives came to see him, and were much troubled, "for they looked upon it to be a great shame, to them, for me to be imprisoned for religion; and some thought I was mad because I stood for purity and righteousness and perfection."

It was during this imprisonment at Derby that the name "Quaker" was first applied to George Fox, because he often exhorted his hearers to quake and fear before the mighty power of God. On some occasions violent tremblings seized the early Friends during their united prayers.

After his discharge from Derby gaol, in 1651, he proceeded to Yorkshire, and preached in various parts of that county, especially in Holderness, the eastern coast, and Cleveland, not fearing to rebuke the "priests" again in their "steeple-houses." Thus, at one place, the clergyman preached from the text, "Ho! every one that thirsteth, come ye to the waters; yea come, buy wine and milk without money and without price." Whereupon George exclaimed, "Come down, thou deceiver. Dost thou bid people come freely, and take of the water of

life freely, and yet thou takest three hundred pounds a
year of them for preaching the Scriptures to them?
Mayest thou not blush for shame?"

Many of the Yorkshire men, especially the intelligent
yeomanry, received George's doctrines willingly, and
became his followers. Others—chiefly of the ignorant
and poorer class—treated him with much cruelty. At one
place he was refused food or lodging at an inn, and
obliged to lie in a haystack all night in the rain and snow,
it being only three days before Christmas. At another
place he was compelled to lodge amongst the furze bushes.
Indeed, at that time he says, " I lay many weeks without
doors."

At Tickhill, near Doncaster, when he began to speak
in the church—not during the service or sermon—he
writes: " They immediately fell upon me, and the clerk
up with his Bible as I was speaking, and struck me on
the face with it, so that my face gushed out with blood,
and I bled exceedingly in the steeple-house. Then the
people cried, ' Let us have him out of the church;' and
when they had got me out they beat me exceedingly, and
threw me down and over a hedge; and afterwards they
dragged me through a house into a street, stoning me and
beating me as they dragged me along, so that I was all
over besmeared with blood and dirt. They took my hat
from me, which I never got again. Yet when I was got
upon my legs again, I declared to them the word of life,
and showed them the fruits of their teacher, and how they
dishonoured Christianity."

Similarly, he was thrust out of Wakefield church on a
Sabbath-day, the people " punching and beating me."

Thereabouts, also, George's lodging accommodation was very comfortless; for one night he and three companions lay in a hedge, and another night in a wood, where, he says, "we were very wet, for it rained exceedingly." Soon afterwards he mentions spending the night on a common, on some fern or bracken.

At York, George went into the fine old Minster, where he was *invited* by the worshippers to speak. He told them that "they lived in words, but God Almighty looked for fruits among them." He says, "As soon as the words were out of my mouth, they hurried me out and threw me down the steps." From Doncaster church also he was hurried out, thrown down, and haled before the magistrates. At Balby he was stoned.

Nevertheless, his preaching was very impressive in general and excited deep thoughtfulness, amongst the yeomanry in particular. Many of the clergy and their hearers were alarmed when the rumour spread that "the man in leathern breeches is come." George records, "At the hearing thereof the priests in many places would get out of the way, they were so struck with the dread of the eternal power of God; and fear surprised the hypocrites."

He had need of leather breeches during the rough travel and whilst lodging in hedges and brakes, to say nothing of the pushings, halings, and violent assaults of his infuriated adversaries in many places. Nothing but the most substantial vestments could keep him in tidy trim amid such experiences.

And, after his reception in the various "steeple-houses," it is no matter of surprise that his associations with ecclesiastical buildings were neither poetical nor reverential.

The fearless boldness and indomitable perseverance of
Fox won him many admirers amongst the soldiers. He
was again and again urged to enter the army, and was
offered the command of a company if he would accept it.
But he repeatedly refused, feeling himself called to fight
with spiritual rather than carnal weapons. The stern,
but honest-hearted Cromwell, recognised the sterling sense
and goodness of George Fox, and, with tears in his eyes,
exclaimed to him after his first interview, "Come again,
come again to my house; for if thou and I were but an
hour of a day together we should be nearer one to the
other." However, Fox was no courtier, and did not seek
for further intimacy with the Protector or his chief men.
Even on this occasion he refused to accept Oliver's kindly-
offered hospitality when invited to dine at Whitehall.
Hereupon the Protector remarked, "Now I see there is
a people risen and come up that I cannot win either with
gifts, honours, offices, or places; but all other sects and
people I can." Fox adds, "It was told him again that
we had forsaken our own, and were not like to look for
such things from him."

Truly a remarkable and unparalleled disinterestedness
characterised George Fox and the early Friends, as was
abundantly evidenced in their lifelong sacrifices for the
Gospel, in the face of tremendous opposition, and without
hope of any earthly reward.

The difficulties of the itinerant ministry of the first
Friends were greatly increased by the absence of roads in
most districts of the kingdom, the small number of inns,
and the extensive tracks of unpeopled wilderness which
then occupied the sites of our modern crowded towns and

fertile estates. Lord Macaulay (speaking of a period forty years later than the rise of Quakerism) says, "Could the England of 1685 be, by some magical process, set before our eyes, we should not know one landscape in a hundred, or one building in ten thousand." "From those books and maps (of the seventeenth century) it is clear that many routes which now pass through an endless succession of orchards, hayfields, and beanfields, then ran through nothing but heath, swamp, and warren." Thousands of deer fed in the forests around London, especially in Enfield Chase. In various parts of the land the sportsmen at times made great massacres of foxes, wild cats, and fen eagles. "On all the downs from the British Channel to Yorkshire huge buzzards strayed in troops of fifty or sixty. The marshes of Cambridge and Lincolnshire were covered during some months of every year by immense clouds of cranes." Salt meat was the general diet of English households in winter; vegetables were few and scarce. The wages of agricultural labourers were four shillings a week. Horses were purchased for about fifty shillings each. Coal was only used in a few places easily accessible from the pits.

Only four provincial towns in England contained at this period as many as 10,000 inhabitants. Many of our populous and busy seats of nineteenth-century industry were then the haunts of wild animals, or, at best, consisted of a few rural cottages. All travel, with the very rare exception of a coach for wealthy ladies, was performed on horseback or on foot, leisurely and with much peril from hindrances of quagmires and floods, to say nothing of freebooters.

The squires were a set of ignorant rustic magnates, little superior (except in wealth) to the poorest of the people. The clergy also were, as a body, very ignorant, and still more bigoted and harsh, except in the Metropolis and the Universities and in the case of a few isolated worthies elsewhere. Intelligence and virtue were mainly to be found amongst the yeomanry or the small freeholders—a much larger body then, in proportion to the population, than they are now—who were, as a class, Nonconformists, and who constituted the strength and flower of the victorious armies of the Commonwealth—the most valiant and most pious legions the world has ever witnessed, and only approached subsequently by the intelligent volunteers sent forth in our own days from the innumerable freehold homes of the United States to maintain the liberties of their great republic against the advocates of a slavery hardly worse in kind than that attempted by Laud and Strafford.

CHAPTER V.

SUCCESS IN THE NORTH—QUAKERISM ESTABLISHED.

IN WESTMORELAND AND LANCASHIRE—FIRBANK CHAPEL—
GAINS NUMEROUS AND ZEALOUS COADJUTORS — ARDUOUS
SERVICE—EIGHTY THOUSAND QUAKERS IN FOX'S DAYS—
POWER OF CONCENTRATED ENERGY — SWARTHMOOR HALL
AND THE FELL FAMILY—MARGARET FELL—CRUEL ASSAULTS
AT ULVERSTONE AND WALNEY ISLAND — MEETS FORTY
PRIESTS AT LANCASTER—LETTER TO SAWREY — IMPRISONED
AT CARLISLE — RETURNS TO THE SOUTHERN COUNTIES AND
TO LONDON.

GEORGE Fox spent three years in the six northern
counties (1651-54); and of this service the most interesting and important was his ministry in the small
district included between Lancaster, Sedberg, Kendal, and
Ulverstone, among the rocky fells looking down on the
pleasant valleys of the Lune and Kent, and on the breezy
waters of Morecambe Bay. This was a locality which
George always loved; here he achieved his greatest
triumphs; here he gained his most enthusiastic converts, both amongst zealous lion-hearted men and kindly
motherly women; here he won his faithful wife Margaret;
here, too, he underwent some of the sharpest persecutions
and imprisonments of his life; hither he repeatedly retired
in later years, to rest awhile from his arduous labours;

here, also, there has remained down to the present day a
company of his most earnest followers.

After his rough experiences in the Yorkshire churches
he traversed the picturesque Wensleydale, Grisedale, and
Lunedale, and thence passed over into Westmoreland.
Here, on the high fells between Kendal and Sedberg, he
preached a sermon memorable in the annals of Quakerism.
It was delivered from the summit of a weather-beaten
rock adjoining the bleak moorland chapel of Firbank,
whither a great company of zealous preachers and laymen
had assembled from all the surrounding district for a
religious conference. George Fox, taking advantage of
the opportunity, came also, and being favourably recommended by several of the audience who had previously
heard him preach, was invited to address the congregation.
In a sermon of three hours' duration he set forth the con-
victions of his heart, and succeeded in communicating his
enthusiasm to many of his hearers, some of whom speedily
devoted themselves to the work of promulgating his views.

Amongst those who, in consequence of this and similar
meetings in this district, became his coadjutors, were some
of the most eminent leaders of the early Friends, and
in particular John Audland, Francis Howgill, Edward
Burrough, and George Whitehead. Edward Burrough
was the Xavier of early Quakerism, a young man of
the most fervent soul, who devoted himself mainly to the
work of preaching in the Metropolis, and, after ten years
of very arduous ministry, died, worn out with labours,
travels, and imprisonments, at the early age of twenty-
eight.

In all, about sixty energetic preachers were the harvest

of this northern journey of George Fox. Many of them were mere youths, but the fervour and prayerful dedication of their hearts gave them the strength of giants in promulgating their principles in the face of innumerable difficulties and of the most bitter persecution. As an illustration of their activity it may be mentioned that young George Whitehead travelled on foot out of Westmoreland, on a preaching journey, at the age of eighteen, and proceeded sixty miles to York; thence, after a stay of three days, he walked on eighty miles to Lincoln, and the next day started for Cambridge, where he arrived in three days, and thence proceeded, again on foot, to Norwich. In this manner Quaker itinerant preachers spread their doctrine over England, Scotland, and Ireland, and in a few years to various parts of the Continent, the West Indies, and the North American colonies.

Although these sixty Quaker pioneers were mostly young and vigorous, the greater part of them — and certainly the most active of them—appear to have died within fifteen years of their commencing the itinerant ministry. They wore out their lives in hardships, imprisonments, and toils, presenting themselves as living sacrifices to their invisible Lord, and preferring the everlasting certainties of faith to the temporary comforts of worldly ease.

The period from 1650 to 1655 witnessed the complete establishment of Quakerism, and probably its *maximum* number of adherents.

For, from the registry of Quaker names who died in London during the great plague, it has been reasonably estimated that there were then 10,000 Friends in the Metropolis alone. And from various data it is similarly

computed that the total number throughout the kingdom, at the same period, was about 80,000. Hence,
George Fox and his coadjutors were remarkably successful, especially when we remember how bitterly they
were persecuted. A harvest of 80,000 followers was
probably nearly as large a proportionate part of the
whole population of the kingdom then as a million
would be at the present day. But from that period the
numbers have, with more or less regularity, continued
to decline, until now, after two centuries of existence,
Quakerism possesses fewer than 15,000 adherents, of
whom barely 2,000 inhabit London and its vicinity. But
whilst the numbers of Quakerism have thus diminished,
its power and influence have increased. The 15,000
now are stronger in some respects than the 80,000
were then.

And there is no prospect whatever of the extinction of
the Society, as some persons imagine. By no means. It
should have learnt the lesson that power for the highest
good may be as largely possessed, and far more effectually
wielded, by a compact disciplined phalanx than by a great
multitude of adherents. By power we would here mean
efficient Christian influence on the world, irrespective of mere
numerical proselytism. For instance, how incomparably
greater has been the influence exercised upon the world by
the small prayerful band of one hundred and twenty
disciples meeting in the upper room at Jerusalem after the
Ascension, than of the ignoble hosts of Israel in the reign
of Solomon, of whom it is simply recorded, that "Judah
and Israel were many, as the sand which is by the sea
in multitude, eating and drinking, and making merry."
(1 Kings iv. 20.)

It is not improbable but that the influence of Quakerism would be still more powerful, and more beneficial than ever, if its ranks were reduced to a half or third of its present numbers by the abolition of the existing system of birthright membership. What would be thus lost in quantity would be gained in quality, in intensity, in enthusiasm, in concentrated vigour of action and influence. Some of the best friends of Quakerism would gladly see its ranks thus further diminished under such salutary conditions.

Amongst the spots often visited by George Fox, in the district we have specially alluded to, was Swarthmoor Hall, near Ulverstone, the seat of Judge Fell, a worthy legal brother and contemporary of Sir Matthew Hale. On the occasion of Fox's first visit there he attended the morning service at Ulverstone church, and, when the clergyman had finished, he asked permission to speak, which was granted. Then, standing on a seat, he preached an impressive sermon on the necessity of heartfelt sincerity in religious profession, and of an individual inward realisation of the things contained in Holy Scripture. Many of his hearers were profoundly moved at this address. One of them was Margaret Fell (the wife of Judge Fell) who writes of the occasion, "I stood up in my pew and wondered at his doctrine; for I had never heard such before." After describing the sermon, she adds, " Then I saw clearly we were all wrong. So I sat down in my pew again, and cried bitterly; and I cried in my spirit to the Lord, ' We have taken the Scriptures in words, and know nothing of them in ourselves.' "

That evening George Fox, by invitation, preached to

the family and servants at Swarthmoor Hall, and with such effect that the whole household became convinced of the truth of his doctrine. Meanwhile, Judge Fell was absent on the Welsh circuit. In three weeks he returned, and was immediately informed by the neighbouring gentry that his family had been " bewitched " by the Quakers in his absence. He was, therefore, greatly annoyed; but his wife sent for George Fox, who was still in the vicinity, to come and explain matters. Accordingly, one evening George came over to the Hall, and Margaret Fell (after having, with womanly tact, first taken care that her husband should have a good supper) introduced him to the Judge. George then set forth his doctrine, and added a severe exposure of the conduct of the clergy in various parts of the country. Margaret Fell thus records the result of this interview: " And so my husband came to see clearly the truth of what he spoke, and was very quiet that night, said no more, and went to bed. The next morning came Lampitt, priest of Ulverstone, and got my husband into the garden and spoke much to him there; but my husband had seen so much the night before that the priest got little entrance upon him." From that time forward the Judge offered no opposition to the Quakerism of his household, but at once gave them and their Friends permission to hold a regular meeting at the Hall, there being no other place in the immediate neighbourhood suitable for a chapel. This meeting continued to be held there for forty years, until 1686, when George Fox built a meeting-house adjoining the Hall and endowed it with three acres of land which he had previously purchased. This Quaker chapel remains, and is still used as such.

On the next Sabbath, after Judge Fell's return, he rode off to Ulverstone church, unattended as hitherto by his family and household, and having merely his clerk and groom with him. He continued a Churchman to the end of his life, but always protected the Quaker element which had so suddenly and so overwhelmingly leavened his establishment. He was a wise and learned man, incorruptible as a judge, honoured and feared as a magistrate, and beloved by his neighbours. He died in 1658, six years after Fox's first visit to Swarthmoor, at the age of sixty. His wife, who had married him at the age of eighteen, was then forty-four. They had lived happily together for twenty-six years, and had one son and seven daughters.

In 1669, eleven years after the Judge's death, George Fox married his widow, he being then forty-five years of age, and she fifty-five. So that Margaret Fox was sixteen years younger than her first husband, and ten years older than her second. She survived the latter eleven years, dying at Swarthmoor on February 2, 1702, aged eighty-eight. Her last words were, " I am in peace." She was a noble, motherly, and godly woman, fair in person, courteous and kindly in manners, and a worthy great-granddaughter of the martyr Anne Askew. Shortly before her decease she remarked to a friend, " The Lord is with me, and I am with the Lord ; and in Him only will I trust, and commit all to the divine providence of the Lord, both concerning my children and grandchildren, and all things they do enjoy from Him, both in spirituals and in naturals, who is the God of all the mercies and blessings to his people, throughout all generations. To Him be glorious

praises for ever." (Quoted in "Journal and Life of
Fox," p. 403.*)

The success of George Fox with Judge Fell and his
family exceedingly enraged the clergy and magistrates of
the neighbourhood; and accordingly they directed the
full vigour of their opposition against the new comer.
The people, instigated by one Justice Sawrey and by
Parson Lampitt, knocked George down, kicked him,
trampled upon him, beat him with stakes and holly-
bushes, and dragged him through the town to a marshy
common, where they left him senseless. Judge Fell's son
ran after them to see what was happening, and the savage
mob threw the youth into a ditch, whilst some cried,
"Knock the teeth out of his head!" When George
recovered his consciousness he began to preach again;
presently he was further assaulted, but nevertheless went
boldly back to Ulverstone Market-place, where a soldier
accosted him, saying, "Sir, I see you are a man, and I am
ashamed and grieved that you should be thus abused;"
hereupon he drew his sword and would have attacked
Fox's foes, but George entreated him to sheath the
weapon. He writes, "My body and arms were yellow,
black, and blue, with the blows and bruises I received
amongst them that day."

A fortnight afterwards George Fox proceeded to Walney
Island, near the adjacent coast, and records, "As soon as
I came to land there rushed out about forty men with
staves, clubs, and fishing-poles, who fell upon me, beating

---

* An interesting biography of Margaret (Fell) Fox and her
family has been written by Maria Webb of Dublin, entitled, "The
Fells of Swarthmoor Hall." London: A. W. Bennett.

and punching me, and endeavouring to thrust me back-
ward into the sea." Here again he was knocked senseless,
and his friends hurried him back in the boat. But they
were between the horns of a dilemma, for he adds, " When
I was come over to the town again, on the other side of
the water, the townsmen rose up with pitchforks, flails,
and staves, to keep me out of the town, crying, ' Kill him,
knock him on the head, bring the cart and carry him away
to the churchyard.' " He was thus driven away from that
place.

Shortly afterwards he was summoned to appear at the
Lancaster Sessions on a charge of blasphemy. Here, he
says, " there appeared against me about forty priests."
The charge could not be sustained, and he achieved a
triumph, having had an excellent opportunity of pro-
claiming his views to a large company of the neighbouring
magistrates, several of whom, including the mayor of
Lancaster, became his converts.

He had now nearly accomplished his campaign in the
Lake district, one attended by remarkable hostility and
still more remarkable success. But, before quitting the
locality, he addressed a few vigorous protests to his worst
persecutors, especially to Lampitt and Sawrey. In these
protests, which George declared he was " moved " to
write, there were some expressions which might appear
uncharitable but for the excessive provocations received.
For instance, he writes to Sawrey, " Thou wast the first
stirrer-up of strikers, stoners, persecutors, mockers, and
imprisoners in the North, and of revilers, slanderers,
railers, and false accusers! How wilt thou be gnawed
and burned one day, when thou shalt feel the flame, and

I

have the plagues of God poured upon thee, and thou
begin to gnaw thy tongue because of the plagues! Thou
shalt have thy reward according to thy works. Thou canst
not escape. The Lord's righteous judgments will find
thee out."

Sawrey was eventually drowned; and it was often
noticed in those days that the cruel persecutors of the
Friends met with violent and untimely deaths. Some of
them, in their last moments, confessed that the Divine
judgments were indeed come upon them for their merciless
deeds.

It is easy now to charge George Fox and his fellow-
sufferers with using language of an unchristian and uncharitable nature; but the provocation was tremendous.
The meekness and forgiveness of the Friends were in
general marvellous. And if, at times, they could not
restrain themselves, the fault was that of their pitiless
foes. Nor is it surprising that they were especially severe
in their protests against the clergy, inasmuch as the latter
made their cruelty immeasurably worse by claiming for it
the sanction and alliance of Divine law.

George Fox now proceeded further north into Cumberland, Durham, and Northumberland. In this district,
again, he met with the Baptists, many of whom became
his followers. At Carlisle he was again imprisoned for
interrupting the services in a church. Some of his fellow-
ministers were also imprisoned at this time.

After his release from Carlisle Gaol he held meetings,
many of which were very large and solemn gatherings,
throughout the neighbouring counties, and everywhere
gained adherents and faithful coadjutors. In 1654 he

concluded his great pioneering work in the north, and departed to Leicestershire, London, and the southern and western counties.

Quakerism was now an established fact. It had taken permanent hold of many of the best men in the nation, and, meanwhile, scores of zealous converts were preaching its doctrines throughout the kingdom.

Henceforth the work of George Fox was rather that of a counsellor and organiser than a pioneer. By 1654 he had fought and won the decisive battles of his life. The remaining ones were of comparatively minor importance.

CHAPTER VI.

DIFFICULTIES AND SEVERE IMPRISONMENTS.

CASE OF JAMES NAYLOR—ITS EFFECT UPON FOX AND THE FRIENDS—MANY FRIENDS IN PRISON—GENERAL MEETINGS —FOX'S EXTENSIVE HOME JOURNEYS—HIS REPEATED IMPRISONMENTS—SPECIALLY OPPOSED BY THE CLERGY—WHITTIER'S LINES—PAROLED AT LANCASTER—SECOND IMPRISONMENT AT LANCASTER—REFUSAL TO TAKE OATHS—SENT TO SCARBOROUGH CASTLE—INTEGRITY—EXTREME WEAKNESS OF BODY AT HIS DISCHARGE—PAROLED AND IMPRISONED AT WORCESTER—FINAL LIBERATION—THOUSANDS OF FRIENDS IMPRISONED—THE WORD OF A KING—FATAL PERSECUTIONS IN NEW ENGLAND—MACAULAY ON CHARLES THE SECOND'S REIGN—PEPYS'S DESCRIPTION OF THE COURT —BISHOP BURNET—FOX AT CAMBRIDGE.

In 1656, a very painful occurrence took place, which brought great sorrow upon the Friends, but which was overruled for salutary effects, both upon George Fox and his followers as a body. One of his converts, named James Naylor, formerly a quarter-master in the parliamentary armies, had preached in various counties with an eloquence which excited much admiration, and which especially fascinated some of his female auditors. Flattered and excited by a few visionary women, poor Naylor yielded to some extraordinary delusions. Having imbibed extreme notions respecting Fox's doctrine of "Christ within," he permitted these flatterers to address him in

terms which were positive blasphemy. Thus, on entering
the city of Bristol, one of the women led his horse, and
the others spread their garments before him, exclaiming
" Holy, holy, holy, is the Lord God of Hosts ! Hosannah
in the highest ! "

This procedure astonished even the people of an age
accustomed to religious extravagances. Naylor, with his
party, was promptly arrested and sent to London, where
his case was brought before Parliament and claimed their
attention for twelve days. His punishment was a severe
one. He was placed in the pillory, whipped through
London (receiving 310 stripes which terribly lacerated his
body), pilloried again, branded on the forehead with a hot
iron, bored through the tongue, then taken to Bristol and
flogged through the streets there, and further imprisoned
for two years. After his discharge, he voluntarily made
public confessions of his sin, manifested the most sincere
repentance, and died in 1660, in a very humble and
contrite state of mind.

George Fox and the other Friends had, previously to
the sad affair at Bristol, warned Naylor and rebuked his
conceit. But the event was useful to Fox himself, inasmuch as that good man also had, on various occasions,
expressed assumptions based on the same doctrine of
" Christ within," which were certainly dangerous.
Further, he had himself been occasionally addressed by
his admirers, especially by some Quaker women, in a style
which was highly objectionable, and even blasphemous, but
which he does not appear to have encouraged.

Poor Naylor's case came upon the Friends as a terrible
warning. The lesson was sharp but salutary, for it

effected a change in the career of Fox and many others.
From that period George Fox's language was more
cautious, his conduct more guarded, his doctrine more
sound and scriptural. And thereafter the dangerous
ambiguities of some other of the Quaker practices appear
to have been greatly lessened. But it may be admitted
that throughout the history of Quakerism, at least till
the *Beaconite* secession of 1836, the weak side of the
Society was its danger of substituting for the Holy
Scriptures the asserted superior certainty and divinity of
inward voices. But the Holy Spirit has not ordained that
any inward manifestation should *take the place* of His
outwardly recorded words of Holy Scripture. The Divine
wisdom of the priceless gift of the Bible is shown by the
fact that *evil* voices, as well as good ones, speak to the
soul of man, and may readily, at times, be mistaken for
the latter, apart from the check and greater clearness
of an outward revelation cognisable by the great body
of manifestly pious believers in the Church Universal.

At the same time this outward revelation, the Bible, is
a treasure which cannot be effectually received, or acted
on without the *additional* reception of the energies, and
holy love to God and man, derived from the actual
presence of the Holy Spirit. No words can too re-
verentially declare the indispensability of the gift and fruit
of this Sacred Spirit in the heart of man. But the weak
side of George Fox and his followers has almost always
been the tendency to confound the *distinctly separate*, but
ever harmonious, offices of the Divine Spirit and those of
the Scriptures, and *to attribute to the former the functions
which He himself has positively committed to the latter.*

This tendency, however, has been accompanied in general by many balancing checks, and notwithstanding its danger, George Fox, at least, *practically* manifested an example of honour to the Bible, and of obedience to its teachings.

By the year 1656 the Friends were so numerous and faithful that there were seldom fewer than a thousand of them in prison during the next four years, chiefly for scruples respecting the payment of tithes, for refusing to go to church, to take oaths, or to uncover their heads before magistrates.

In 1656, three General Meetings of Friends, from various parts of the nation, assembled at Balby in York-shire, Ringwood in Hampshire, and Exeter in Devon. These were large and solemn gatherings, and resulted in valuable conferences and renewed energies. In 1658, a General Meeting, held at Skipton in Yorkshire, issued orders to raise funds annually for the payment of the expenses of travelling ministers. Hitherto such had usually defrayed their own expenses. This has often been the case subsequently. But, as a general rule, expenses of ministers' transit are paid by the Society. At this Skipton Meeting £443 was contributed on the spot, a very large collection in those days. At another General Meeting at Skipton in 1660, a renewed appeal was issued for funds to aid Quaker ministers then travelling in Germany, America, Tuscany, Lombardy, the Palatinate, Rome, Turkey, Jerusalem, France, Switzerland, Norway, Bar-badoes, the Bermudas, Jamaica, Surinan, and Newfound-land.

During the twenty-five years following his first northern

journey, George Fox continued his itinerant mission-work with unremitting perseverance. In this period he traversed England (repeatedly), Scotland, Ireland, and Wales. He spent two years in the West Indies and the North American Colonies, was four times at the Land's End, many times at Swarthmoor and the Lancaster district, and still more frequently in London. He sometimes visited the greater part of England in a single year, as in 1656, in 1663, in 1666, and again in 1668. In this marvellous energy he resembled Wesley and Whitfield ; but, in the time of the latter, travelling was very much more easy than in Fox's days. The founders of Methodism had some persecution to encounter, but it was insignificant compared with the long-sustained, barbarous, and often fatal onslaughts made upon the English Nonconformists and Scotch Covenanters in the preceding century.

Thus, in 1656, George Fox was imprisoned eight months in Launceston Castle, in a filthy dungeon, deep in mire ; in 1660 he was imprisoned in Lancaster Castle ; in 1664-6 he was again confined for two years in Lancaster and Scarborough Castles ; and in 1674-5 he was imprisoned for fourteen months at Worcester. On each of these occasions he was punished on *false* charges of intended insurrection, or for harmless conscientious scruples, such as refusing to take oaths, or uncover his head before the authorities. And, in general, clergymen were his bitterest foes and the fiercest in hounding on the civil power upon him.

Well and justly has the Quaker poet Whittier, in his poem on Clerical Advocacy of the Gallows, alluded to this often-manifested scandal of ministerial severity in

former ages, and to its continuance in our own days, when
so many thousand sermons, based on isolated texts (interpreted contrary to the general scope and spirit of Christianity, just as Satan quoted Scripture to tempt our
Saviour), have been preached in vindication of slavery
(because Paul sent back Onesimus), war, the gallows, and
the administration of a stern and inconsiderately rigid
treatment of criminals and paupers, irrespective of their
usual antecedents and often irresistible temptations. It is
a grievous scandal this; even to-day, clergymen and
ministers are too often found sneering at philanthropy
and social science reforms, as "humanitarianism" and as
"sentimentalism." Whittier reminds us that—

> "Where Christ hath spoken peace, His name hath been
> The loudest war-cry of contending men;
> Priests, pale with vigils, in His name have blessed
> The unsheathed sword, and laid the spear in rest,
> Wet the war-banner with their sacred wine,
> And crossed its blazon with the holy sign;
> Yea, in His name who bade the erring live,
> And daily taught the lesson—to forgive,
> Twisted the cord and edged the murderous steel;
> And with His words of mercy on their lips
> Hung gloating o'er the pincers' burning grips
> And the grim horror of the straining wheel.
>
> *　　*　　*　　*　　*
>
> The midnight of Bartholomew,—the stake
> Of Smithfield, and that thrice-accursed flame
> Which Calvin kindled by Geneva's lake—
> New England's scaffold, and the priestly sneer,
> Which marked its victims in that hour of fear;
> When guilt itself a human tear might claim,
> Bear witness, O Thou wronged and merciful One!
> That Earth's *most hateful crimes* have *in Thy name*
>   been done!"

There are some of the noblest men upon earth to
be found amongst the ranks of the priesthood, both of Rome
and of England; nevertheless, too many of their clerical
brethren have distorted the Scriptures of the God of love
to support arguments in favour of objects diametrically
opposed to the spirit of the Bible. Thus, only a few
months ago, an ecclesiastical dignitary of Westminster
Abbey preached a sermon to associate the hangman with
the odour of sanctity !

As an illustration of the utterly malicious nature of
much of the persecution inflicted upon George Fox, it may
be mentioned that when he was imprisoned in Lancaster,
in 1660, the charge laid against him in the mittimus was,
"that he, with others, had endeavoured to raise insurrection and embroil the whole country in blood."
He replied, "I was never an enemy to the king nor
to any man's person upon earth." Some of his friends in
London procured a writ of Habeas Corpus requiring him
to be brought thither for trial. Hereupon the Sheriff of
Lancaster, in order to spare the expense of conducting his
prisoner to London, liberated him, upon his simple promise
to appear before the judges in town on a certain day!
Accordingly Fox proceeded to London, holding meetings
by the way, and in due time surrendered himself there in
court. When the judges and lawyers heard the charges
read, describing him as such a dangerous personage, seeking to embroil the nation in blood, and further learnt that
he had been permitted to travel *without guard or restraint*
250 miles, under the writ of Habeas Corpus, the glaring
inconsistency of thus paroling a prisoner, committed on such
a charge, so astonished and amused them, that they lifted

their hands in amazement. Further, none of his accusers appeared against him, and the King promptly issued an order for his release. He records of this discharge, "After it was known that I was discharged, a company of envious wicked spirits were troubled, and terror took hold of Justice Porter [on whose warrant he had been committed to Lancaster Castle and detained there five months], for he was afraid I would take the advantage of the law against him for my wrong imprisonment, and thereby undo him, his wife and children. And, indeed, I was pressed by some in authority to have made him and the rest examples, but I said I should leave them to the Lord; if the Lord forgave them, I should not trouble myself with them."

George Fox's second imprisonment at Lancaster Castle, in 1664, was a time of terrible suffering. (The brave-hearted Margaret Fell, his future wife, was imprisoned in the same building at that time, and for four years altogether, for refusing to take an oath.) George also was confined for the same offence, and for being a "rebel" and dangerous character. Yet, on this occasion, also, the magistrates, when committing him for trial, had liberated him on his parole until the assizes, when he faithfully delivered himself up. At his trial, his shrewdness and acumen were displayed by his discovery of four flaws in the indictment, each one sufficient in equity to upset it. The judge, in anger, exclaimed, "You are at liberty; but I will put the oath to you again!" Whereupon a Bible was tendered him to swear upon. George protested that that very book commanded, "Swear not at all." He added, "I never took an oath, covenant or engagement in my life;

but my yea and nay were more binding in me than an oath was to many others. I was a man of tender conscience, and it was in obedience to Christ's command that I could not swear." This plea did not avail him, but he was consigned to prison. He records, "Yet this got about all over the country as a by-word, 'That they gave me a book to swear on that commanded me not to swear at all, and the Bible was at liberty, and I in prison for doing what the Bible said.'"

He was confined all the following winter in a tower which was constantly filled with smoke from the prison fires, and where the wind and rain also came in freely and could not be kept out. His swelled limbs evinced the acuteness of his sufferings.

At the next assizes he again detected several flaws in the new indictment, but was recommitted and sentenced to a premunire,* which involved perpetual imprisonment. After some time he was transferred from Lancaster to Scarborough Castle in Yorkshire, and there placed in a room with no fireplace and open to the rain and storm. He describes it thus: "This room being to the seaside, and lying much open, the wind drove in the rain forcibly, so that the rain came over my bed and ran about the room, that I was fain to skim it up with a platter. And when my clothes were wet I had no fire to dry them; so that my body was benumbed with cold and my fingers swelled, that one was grown as big as two." His friends were forbidden to bring him food or comforts. He says, "Commonly a threepenny loaf served me three weeks, and sometimes longer, and most of my drink was water with wormwood steeped or bruised in it."

Truly has Macaulay written of those days, " The prisons were hells on earth, seminaries of every crime and of every disease. At the assizes the lean and yellow culprits brought with them from their cells to the dock an atmosphere of stench and pestilence which sometimes avenged them signally on bench, bar, and jury."

After two years' continuous imprisonment, George Fox was liberated from Scarborough by an order from the King, procured mainly through a friend at court, one " Esquire Marsh," by whom he had long been known and appreciated, and who now declared that, if necessary, " he would go a hundred miles barefoot for the liberty of George Fox." The Governor of the Castle, who had at first treated him cruelly, gradually conceived a respect and esteem for his harmless honest-hearted prisoner. Ever afterwards he protected the Friends as much as he could. (When, several years later, George Fox again visited Scarborough, the Governor invited him to his residence and treated him with the greatest courtesy.) The soldiers and officers, who had been severe to George at first, said of him at his discharge, " He is as stiff as a tree, and as pure as a bell, for we could never bow him."

He was now so very weak in body, when liberated, that it appeared unlikely that he could long survive. He was only able to travel a mile or two in a day for some time afterward.

His next imprisonment (of fourteen months) was at Worcester, in 1674. A clergyman there complained bitterly that through the preaching of Fox he had lost nearly all the attenders of his church. Whereupon he prevailed upon the authorities to tender the oath of allegiance, previously knowing Fox's scruples against taking it. Again his friends procured a writ of Habeas Corpus to bring him to London, and the Sheriff of Worcester permitted him to go up on parole. In London he was, through some technical difficulty, remanded to Worcester, but the judge permitted him to be again at liberty on his promise to appear at the following assizes there. Here he was once more paroled till a future trial. Eventually he was consigned to prison; and during his confinement his beloved aged mother died, her end being hastened by bitter sorrow at her son's inability to come and take leave of her. In 1675, George Fox was once more removed to London by Habeas Corpus; this time his indictment was found to be so full of errors that it was immediately quashed. Some of his enemies protested against his liberation, alleging that he was "a dangerous man," to which Lord Chief Justice Hale replied, that "he had indeed heard some such reports, but he had also heard many more good reports of him." George Fox was, therefore, liberated, and during the remaining fifteen years of his life was permitted to remain in peace, unmolested by gaolers, writs, or assizes.

Thousands of his friends suffered during the reign of Charles the Second. That king, on his accession, had promised a Friend (Richard Hubberthorn), "None of you shall suffer for your opinions or religion, so long as you live peaceably; and you have the word of a king for it." What "the word of a king" was in a Stuart's mouth had been too often proved in Charles the First's days. And now, in his son's reign, there were, *within one year of the above promise,* 4,230 Friends committed to prison in-

nocent of crime or violence!   Many of these died in their
bonds.

Meanwhile, across the Atlantic, some of the Puritans
had set up a State-church in New England, and enforced
compliance by fines, imprisonments and whippings.   (Mr.
Benjamin Scott, Chamberlain of London, has shown in a
recent pamphlet (published by Bennett, London) that
these persecuting Puritans of Boston were not of " the
Pilgrim Father" stock.   They were Episcopalians and not
Nonconformists.)   Finding these measures insufficient to
deter the Friends, they hanged four of them.   On hearing
of this cruelty, the English Friends immediately sent
a deputation to the King to plead for his interposition.
Charles promptly granted a mandamus to stop such proceedings, and, further, entrusted it to a Friend, named
Samuel Shattock, who was in England, having been
banished from New England on pain of death if he
returned.   To the great chagrin of the colonial authorities
he now returned as a Royal Commissioner, armed with a
document overturning their own power in the matter.   It
was a bitter pill to swallow; but the Friends remaining in
prison in the colony were forthwith liberated, and in
future were permitted the exercise of their religion.

King Charles would not have sanctioned the severities
which characterised his reign, in England, had he not
been over-persuaded by the clergy.   Sometimes he
plainly expressed his sense of their evil ways.   Thus, in
1667, in addressing the Privy Council relative to the
disorders of the times, he stated (as Bishop Burnet
admits) that " the clergy were chiefly to blame for these
disorders, for if they had lived well and gone about their

parishes, and taken pains to convince the Nonconformists, the nation might have been by that time well settled. But they thought of nothing but to get good benefices and to keep a good table."

The times were indeed awful. Licentiousness, hypocrisy, and cruelty were rampant. Scotland's fair landscapes were the scenes of martyrdom and butchery, and in England 2,000 of the most virtuous ministers, the flower of the age, were driven into nonconformity and penury. Many thousands more of the excellent of the land were immured in dungeons, tortured, starved, or hanged. Not too severely has Macaulay thus summarised this reign :—

" Then came those days never to be recalled without a blush, the days of servitude without loyalty, and sensuality without love, of dwarfish talents and gigantic vices, the paradise of cold hearts and narrow minds, the golden age of the coward, the bigot, and the slave. The King cringed to his rival, that he might trample on his people; sank into a viceroy of France, and pocketed, with complacent infamy, her degrading insults and her more degrading gold. The caresses of harlots and the jests of buffoons regulated the policy of the state. The government had just ability enough to deceive, and just religion enough to persecute. The principles of liberty were the scoff of every grinning courtier, and the Anathema Maranatha of every fawning dean. Crime succeeded to crime, and disgrace to disgrace, till the race, accursed of God and man, was a second time driven forth to wander on the face of the earth, and to be a by-word and a shaking of the head to the nations."

What contrasts, again, are afforded by the memorials of holy Covenanters and Nonconformists of that day, as compared with the records of the Court and the hierarchy ! Thus Pepys writes of a banquet at Whitehall, in April, 1667 :—" The cheer was extraordinary; each knight having 40 dishes to his mess, piled up five or six feet high; the room hung with the richest tapestry." And, side by side with records of the king's intrigues and profanities, we have descriptions of the sacrament being administered, with full ceremonial, to him and his three illegitimate sons, by the Bishops of London, Durham, and Rochester ! When, a year or two afterwards, the condemned Duke of Monmouth asked for the sacrament, it was refused him, for his immorality ! A king might sin a thousandfold, and yet receive, through episcopal " channels of grace," the rite which was asserted to confer " communion" with the awful and holy One, who, to the persistently wicked (whether king, bishop, or pauper) ever proclaims Himself to be " a consuming fire," an unreconciled and retributive Judge. But to the fallen unsuccessful sinner, " the Church " was " faithful " in its protest against his evil ways.

Bishop Burnet, in describing Charles's primate, Archbishop Sheldon, says, " He seemed not to have a deep sense of religion, *if any at all;* and spoke of it most commonly as an engine of government and a matter of policy." Burnet adds that when the Earl of Clarendon urged the King to do justice to the Dissenters, " the bishops did not approve of it." Here again we are reminded that " The church religious is one thing; the church political is *another.*"

K

When the intolerance of the senior and higher clergy was so excessive, it was not surprising that the University students should display the same disposition. Thus when George Fox visited Cambridge, the young collegians assaulted him as he entered the town, and unhorsed his companion. He records of them—"When we were in the inn they were so rude in the courts and in the streets, that the miners, the colliers, and carters could never be ruder. The people of the house asked us, ' what we would have for supper ? ' ' Supper !' said I ; ' were it not that the Lord's power is over them, these rude scholars look as if they would pluck us in pieces and make a supper of us.' "

CHAPTER VII.

FOX'S FOREIGN MISSION JOURNEYS.

SAILS FOR AMERICA—ESCAPES THE PIRATES—JUDGMENT ON
AN OPPOSER—BARBADOES—COASTS OF VIRGINIA—LARGE
MEETINGS—RHODE ISLAND—FREEDOM OF MINISTRY—ROGER
WILLIAMS AND THE FRIENDS—FOX RETURNS TO ENGLAND—
HIS RETROSPECT OF AMERICAN TRAVEL—VISITS HOLLAND
AND GERMANY—SECOND JOURNEY TO HOLLAND—PROGRESS
OF QUAKERISM ABROAD.

In Fox's foreign travels he underwent many perils and
hardships; but, at the same time, received more general
kindness and courtesy from all classes than in his own
country.

Twelve of his fellow-preachers accompanied him on his
voyage to the West Indies and North America in 1671.
On the voyage they were chased by Barbary pirates, who
overtook them, and appeared to be on the point of attacking
their yacht; but unexpectedly desisted, to the great joy
and surprise of the captain and crew. Fox says for
himself and his companions, " Friends were well satisfied
in themselves, having faith in God, and no fear upon their
spirits." They sought the Lord's protection, and it was
granted. Some weeks afterwards, at Barbadoes, a Barbary merchant gave information that one of the pirate

ships of his people had chased a large yacht at sea, "and were just upon her; but there was a spirit in her that they could not take."

Some years before George Fox visited Barbadoes, a wealthy young man of that island, during a visit to England, fell in love with a rich Quaker orphan girl, who had been placed under the guardianship of George Fox by her mother. He accordingly applied to Fox for his consent to the marriage. The latter refused, saying that the girl's mother had specially desired that her daughter might be trained up in the fear of the Lord. He added, "and therefore I should betray the trust reposed in me if I should consent that he who was out of the fear of God should marry her." The young man, who was "a common swearer and a bad man," was exceedingly angry. When, after his return to Barbadoes, he heard of the expected arrival of George Fox in the island, he repeatedly swore, "I'll have him burned!" George Fox records, "About ten days after, he was struck with a violent burning fever, of which he died, and by which his body was so scorched that the people said 'it was as black as a coal.' Three days before I landed, his body was laid in the dust."

George Fox's transatlantic visit was of great service in organising the numerous Friends previously gathered by earlier Quaker preachers. He everywhere assisted in the establishment of disciplinary meetings and administrative rules. The humane treatment of negroes and Indians claimed much of his attention. He visited some of the Indian tribes in the forests, and held meetings amongst them to mutual satisfaction.

In the then primitive condition of the American colonies travelling was arduous work, involving constant camping out at night, fording deep rivers, wading through swamps and quagmires, and penetrating vast wildernesses. Thus, whilst coasting amongst the bays and rivers of Virginia, he records,—" Being got to land we made a fire in the woods to warm and dry us, and there we lay all that night, the wolves howling about us. Next day we sailed again; but, the wind being against us, we made but little way, and were fain to get to shore at Point Comfort, where yet we found but small comfort; for the weather was so cold that, though we made a good fire in the woods to lie by, our water that we had got for our own use was frozen near the fire-side. We made to sea again the next day; but, the wind being strong and against us, we advanced but little, but were glad to get to land again and travel about to find some house where we might buy some provisions; for our store was spent. That night, also, we lay in the woods; and so extremely cold was the weather, the wind blowing high, and the frost and snow being great, that it was hard for some to abide it." In other places they were pestered with mosquitoes. In the log-houses of the colonists they received a hearty welcome; but even here they often spent the night lying in their clothes by the fires of pine-knots.

In several of the colonies George Fox attended large General Meetings and Yearly Meetings of the district.

In Rhode Island he met with a special welcome. Some of the magistrates there said that if they had money enough they would hire him to be their resident minister. On hearing this, he remarked, " It was time for me to be gone; for if their eye was so much to me, or any of us, they would not come to their own Teacher. For this thing [hiring ministers] had spoiled many, by *hindering them from improving their own talents;* whereas our labour is to bring every one to his own Teacher *in* himself."

This was very honourable and disinterested. But it is to be wished that George Fox and the Friends had confined themselves to the encouragement of the cultivation of individual gifts, without proceeding further to stigmatise all paid preachers as "hireling ministers," to use their favourite term. The establishment of settled pastorates, in *addition* to individual freedom of religious function, has been found to be a necessity, in every age of the Church universal, for the great *masses* of mankind. Small select bodies of "ready-made" Christians, all educated and subjected to a carefully-maintained church discipline, as amongst the Friends and Plymouth Brethren, do not need the care of permanent pastors. Each member is a priest. And this condition of things is eminently favourable to the development of the *highest* form of individual energy and usefulness, both religious and philanthropic. Quakerism is a standing proof of this.

But Quakerism is also a standing proof that its own system is utterly unadapted for the unconverted and ignorant *masses* of mankind. It is admirable for the prepared few, a failure as to the untrained many.

Nevertheless, it is also plain that the testimonies of Fox and the Friends against the "one man system" of ministry have been, and are still, a valuable protest against the *opposite extremes* of hierarchical and ritualistic assumptions. In an age when there are renewed assertions that priests, possessing alleged Apostolical succession, are the exclusive "channels" of the Holy Ghost, even though some of these priests and the recipients of their "gifts" may be manifestly unconverted, supercilious, and destitute of many of the biblical "fruits" and tests of the Divine Spirit, there is a real value in the doctrines of Quakerism on these points. The latter are a useful counterpoise, especially when supported by the holy lives of so many of the Friends holding them.

The Friends have ever held firmly by the ancient, divine, and common-sense rule, " *a tree is known by its fruits.*" They justly refuse to believe in the impartation or presence of invisible spiritual "graces" where there is not the external proof and evidence of their presence.

Again, there is still a high value in the Quaker testimony against the prominence of the money element in the churches. The *Spectator* has recently complained, with truth, that "the principle of the Church of England seems to be, that unless a man is wealthy enough to pay for a University education, he cannot possibly be fit to preach the Gospel to others." In fact, the Anglican Establishment virtually says—" It never pleases God to call a man to the ministry except he has so many hundred pounds to pay for the preliminary expenses virtually imposed by our bishops." Or, at least, "If God does call a man to the office, our bishops will not recognise his call as valid, apart from the outlay of a considerable sum of money." Is this a scriptural state of affairs? Is this a proof of " apostolic succession"?

Whilst in Rhode Island, George Fox and his companions met with an opponent in the eminent and undoubtedly godly Roger Williams, one of the chief founders of that colony. He objected to the theology of Fox as obscuring the fulness and freedom of the pardoning love of God in the Lord Jesus. Having vainly sought for an opportunity of arguing in person with George Fox, he wrote a book of fourteen theses, quaintly entitled (after the manner of the age) " George Fox digged out of his Burrowes," Boston, 1676. In the preface he thus explains its object :

" To the people called Quakers.

" Friends and countrymen. From my childhood, now above threescore years, the Father of lights and mercies touched my soul with a love to Himself, to His only begotten Son, the true Lord Jesus, and to His Holy Spirit," &c. Then, after describing his experiences, he adds—" My conclusion is that, ' Be of good cheer, thy sins are forgiven thee' (Matt. ix.), is one of the joyfullest sounds that ever came to poor sinful ears. How to obtain that sound from the mouth of that Mediator that spoke it is the great dispute between the Protestants and the Romanists. This is also the great point between the true Protestants and yourselves."

Eventually, three of the companions of George Fox (Edmundson, Stubbs, and Burnyeat), had a public dispute with Roger Williams, but it was a very unsatisfactory one. Williams states, respecting it, " My disadvantages in our contests, especially at Newport, were great and many ; for though John Stubbs and John Burnyeat were more civil and ingenious, yet William Edmundson was nothing but a bundle of ignorance and boisterousness; he would speak first and all, though all three were constantly on me at once," &c.

There appears to have been fair ground of complaint as to the want of courtesy towards Williams, and, at an adjourned discussion, this overbearing treatment was still further manifested; insomuch that at length "stood up Captain John Green, one of our magistrates, who observing the insulting carriage, especially of W. Edmundson, he desired leave to propose one query, which being granted, he said he spake not as a magistrate with authority, but as an auditor and sitter-by; and he said, 'I desire to know whether Mr. Williams be here as a delinquent, charged to answer at the bar, or as a disputant upon equal terms?'"

George Fox's return voyage from America was a very tempestuous one. Yet he thankfully records, "The same good hand of Providence that went with us and carried us safely over, watched over us in our return, and brought us safely back again. Thanksgiving and praises be to His holy name for ever. Many sweet and precious meetings we had on board the ship during this voyage (commonly two a week), wherein the blessed presence of the Lord did greatly refresh us, and often break in upon and under the company. When we came into Bristol harbour there lay a man-of-war, and the press-master came on board to impress our men. We had a meeting at that time in the ship with the seamen, before we went to shore; and the press-master sat down with us, stayed the meeting, and was well satisfied with it. After the meeting, I spoke to him to leave two of the men he had impressed in our ship (for he had impressed four), one of which was a lame man : he said, 'at my request he would.'"

This American journey occupied two years. George Fox thus summarises it in one of his letters, dated 1672 : —" We have had great travail by land and sea, and rivers and bays and creeks, in New England, New Jersey, Delaware, Maryland, Virginia, Carolina ; where we have had great service among Friends and governors and others, and with the Indians and their king and emperor. Oh ! blessed be the Lord God Almighty, who is over all, and over all giveth dominion : and glory be to His great Name for ever. Amen."

In 1677, in company with William Penn and Robert Barclay, the two most eminent of the Quakers, except himself, George Fox spent several months preaching in Holland and Germany. At that time there were already many Friends in various parts of the Continent. At Amsterdam, monthly and quarterly "meetings for discipline" had been established, and it was now resolved to institute a Yearly Meeting "for Friends in all the United Provinces of Holland, Embden, the Palatinate, Hamburg, Frederickstadt, Dantzic, and other places in Germany."

During this journey, George Fox held many meetings with the Friends and others. On arriving at towns he used to inquire "whether there were any tender people in the town that feared God, or that had a mind to discourse of the things of God." His interpreter on such occasions was a Dutch Quaker, named John Claus.

In 1684 he paid a second very brief visit to Holland.

Quakerism has now died out in Holland. The writer well remembers the last representative of the Dutch

Friends, a venerable man named John S. Mollett, of Amsterdam. There are a few Friends at Pyrmont and Minden in Germany, and a few at Paris, Nismes, Congenies, and elsewhere in the South of France. In Norway there are several hundreds; but scarcely any in other parts of the Continent.

In the United States—especially in Ohio, Indiana, Illinois, Iowa, and Kansas—the Friends are rapidly increasing in numbers, and already form an aggregate of several hundred thousand.

CHAPTER VIII.

PRIVATE LIFE AND PERSONAL CHARACTERISTICS OF FOX.

HIS MARRIAGE—DISINTERESTED CONDUCT—HIS AFFECTION AS A HUSBAND AND A RELATIVE—MARGARET FOX'S MATRONLY CARE FOR HER HUSBAND—HIS CARE FOR HER—HIS PROPERTY—FOX'S PERSONAL APPEARANCE—HIS PIERCING EYES, POWERFUL VOICE, BODILY STRENGTH, AND SWIFTNESS—HIS TWO PORTRAITS — HIS APPAREL—VERY TEMPERATE—INSTANCES OF HIS SHREWDNESS—KNOWLEDGE OF NATURAL THINGS—APPRECIATION OF SYMBOLISM—HIS SOUND JUDGMENT—COURAGEOUS, CHEERFUL, AND ENERGETIC—HIS PRAYERFUL VIGILANCE AND SERIOUSNESS — REVEREND BUFFOONS—FOX REMARKABLY CONVERSANT WITH THE SCRIPTURES—NOT ELOQUENT.

GEORGE Fox's marriage with the widow of Judge Fell occasioned very little interruption to his ministerial activity. After a brief "honeymoon" of ten days, he again started on a religious journey through the southern counties, and thence to London. Meanwhile his wife returned to Swarthmoor. She had but recently been liberated from four years' imprisonment in Lancaster Castle (for refusing to take an oath). A few months after her marriage, her adversaries again arrested her, and re-committed her, at the age of fifty-six to Lancaster Castle. But good interest was made in her behalf with the king, who soon issued his mandate for her liberation, accompanying it with " a discharge under the broad seal to clear both her and her estate." The remaining thirty-one years of her life were spent in tranquillity, or at least undisturbed by imprisonments or forfeitures of estate.

George Fox's conduct in respect to his marriage was highly honourable and disinterested. Before coming to a conclusion, he consulted the seven daughters of his intended wife, and also her sons-in-law, and obtained their cordial sanction of the proposal. He also took care that the provision for these children of Judge Fell was thoroughly settled and secured before the marriage. The Judge's son was the only member of the family who disapproved of the union; but, inasmuch as he had become a wild and irreligious young man, his opinion was of little, if any, importance, and was, therefore, very properly disregarded.

George Fox, after describing his conference with Margaret Fell's family, respecting the proposed union, adds, " I told them, ' I was plain, and would have all things done plainly; for I sought not any outward advantage to myself.' So after I had thus acquainted the children with it, our intention of marriage was laid before Friends, both privately and publicly, to the full satisfaction of Friends, many of whom gave testimony thereunto that it was of God. Afterwards, a meeting being appointed on purpose for the accomplishing thereof, in the public meeting-house at Broadmead, in Bristol, we took each other in marriage, the Lord joining us together."

About twelve years after this union, on the occasion
of George Fox having to appear in a court of law relative
to a claim on the estate of Swarthmoor for small tithes,
William Mead, who had married one of Judge Fell's
daughters, informed the court that "George Fox had,
before marriage, engaged himself not to meddle with his
wife's estate." The judges present could scarcely believe
in such disinterested conduct, until documents in proof
of it were produced.

George and Margaret Fox's union was, throughout,
a happy and affectionate one. Their mutual love was
eminently accompanied by that which the poet Cowper
describes as an essential element of the truest and best
attachments, whether conjugal or social—

> " Religion ruling in the breast
> A principal ingredient."

After the decease of Fox, his widow, writing a narrative
of the persecutions he had suffered, commences with these
words: " It pleased Almighty God to take away my dear
husband out of this evil troublesome world, who was not
a man thereof, being chosen out of it; who had his life
and being in another region, and whose testimony was
against the world, that the deeds thereof were evil, and
therefore the world hated him." At the age of seventy-
seven, Margaret Fox undertook the then very arduous
journey from Swarthmoor to London (250 miles), to visit
her husband, who had been prostrated by illness whilst
continuing his diligence in the oversight of the numerous
charities established through his influence. In mentioning
this undertaking as " that great journey," the good woman

adds, " I look upon it that the Lord's special hand was in it that I should go then, for he lived but about half a year after I left him; which makes me admire the wisdom and goodness of God in ordering my journey at that time."

Twelve other members of the Fell family also wrote respecting George Fox after his decease. " Neither days nor length of time with us can wear out the memory of our dear and honoured father, George Fox, who, as a tender father to his children (in which capacity we stood, being so related unto him), never failed to give us his wholesome counsel and advice. And not only so, but as a father in Christ he took care of the whole family and household of faith, which the Lord had made him an eminent overseer of."

Twice after his marriage, George Fox was able to spend two years uninterruptedly at Swarthmoor with his wife. On other occasions his visits to his northern home were of short duration. His early covenant with the Lord continued throughout life to be the paramount affection of his spirit, his truly deep affection for his wife not excepted. Even at the close he was far distant from her. But whenever opportunities for manifestations of their mutual love and sympathy occurred, they were promptly and eagerly seized by both. Thus, on the occasion of Margaret Fox's brief but vexatious imprisonment at Lancaster, soon after her marriage, her husband vigorously and efficaciously exerted himself to procure a royal mandate for her liberation.

When, in 1674, he was imprisoned at Worcester, his faithful wife travelled thither from the North to be near

him, and to wait upon him as much as possible. Shortly
afterwards she proceeded to London, and interceded with
the king on his behalf. Charles was willing to grant
a free pardon; but Fox would not accept of his liberation on these or any terms acknowledging him as a
delinquent. He was eventually liberated by the quashing
of his indictment.

During his absences from Swarthmoor he vigilantly
watched over his wife's interests, and took measures to
protect her from the persecutions of some of the neighbouring clergy and magistrates. A letter written from
London, August 8th, 1681, relative to one of these
injuries, commences thus: "Dearly beloved,—There is a
rumour here that one of the Justice Kirbys (but which I
cannot tell) took one of our fat oxen and killed him for
his own table, in his own house, which ox was distrained
and taken away from thee on account of your meeting at
Swarthmoor. Now of the truth of this I desire to know,
and with a witness or two to prove it; for justices of peace
do not deny appeals here." He then requests a minute
specification of all the circumstances, with particular
reference to the terms of certain Acts of Parliament which
he mentions. He concludes his letter with the words—
" Therefore, sweetheart, I do entreat thee let me soon
know the truth of all these things, and what thou writes
let it be proved by witnesses. Thy faithful husband,
George Fox. P.S. The Lord preserve thy soul in patience
through all thy sufferings, troubles, and trials."

This excellent couple were also watchful over one
another's comfort in smaller matters. In " The Fells of
Swarthmoor" it is stated of George Fox that if, when

he was from home, his wife sent him money, it seems he was sure to lay out full as much, or more, in a present for her. Thus, on one occasion, he tells her that with the money she had given him to buy clothes for himself, he had purchased of Richard Smith a piece of red cloth for a mantle, believing she required that more than he needed the coat. And in one of his letters, written to his wife from Worcester prison, he tells her he had got a friend to purchase as much black Spanish cloth as would make her a gown, with what she had given him, adding, " It cost a great deal of money, but I will save.' " From incidental allusions to presents of salmon, &c., sent from Swarthmoor to George Fox, it is evident that, on the other hand, his personal comforts were a matter of great interest to his loving partner.

George Fox derived from his own family and patrimonial property an income sufficient for his personal support. Although not actively taking part in any business, he held shares in two vessels trading from Scarborough, and had an interest in some other undertakings also. From his letters we gather that he had money lodged in the hands of various Friends. Further, a grant of a thousand acres of land in Pennsylvania had been presented to him by William Penn, but he does not appear to have received any income from this latter source.

The personal appearance of George Fox was dignified and portly. His friend, William Penn, describes him as being " a bulky person." Gerard Croese speaks of him as " a large and succulent man." Penn also says of him, " his very presence expressed a religious majesty." He adds : " The inwardness and weight of his spirit, the

L

reverence and solemnity of his address and behaviour, and
the fewness and fulness of his words, have often struck
even strangers with admiration, as they used to reach
others with consolation. The most awful, living, reverent
frame I ever felt or beheld, I must say, was his in prayer.
And truly it was a testimony he knew and lived nearer to
the Lord than other men; for they that know Him most
will see most reason to approach Him with reverence and
fear.

"He was of an innocent life, no busy-body nor self-
seeker, neither touchy nor critical. So meek, contented,
modest, easy, steady, tender, it was a pleasure to be in
his company. A most merciful man, as ready to forgive
as unapt to give or take offence. Civil beyond all forms
of breeding in his behaviour; very temperate, eating little
and sleeping less."

Thomas Ellwood (the friend of Milton) describes Fox
as being "graceful in countenance, manly in personage,
grave in gesture, courteous in conversation, instructive in
discourse, free from affectation in speech or carriage."

His eyes were peculiarly bright and piercing. When
preaching in Holland, a Mennonite minister requested
him to keep his eyes off him, "for they pierced him."
Again, at Carlisle, a Baptist deacon said to him, "Do not
pierce me so with thy eyes; keep thy eyes off me." One
of his gaolers also told him not to look at him so pierc-
ingly. Sometimes, as he walked along, people would
exclaim, "Look at his eyes!" Even judges on the bench
would flinch beneath their powerful glances. His hair was
thick, long, and inclined to curl. In this respect (as in
his dress also) he appears to have affected no needless

eccentricity. The Puritans generally held long hair in abhorrence. He mentions that when many persons complained of the length of his hair, he replied that inasmuch as God had given it to him, and as he felt no pride in its growth, he should allow it to remain.

His voice was an unusually powerful one, and enabled him to command attention even in noisy and tumultuous assemblies. A judge once exclaimed to him in court, " Thou hast good lungs; I must have four or five town-criers in to drown thy voice." When confined in Carlisle gaol (in 1653) the gaoler brought a fiddler to annoy George with his noise, but the latter raised his voice and sung so loudly that, he says, " My voice drowned the noise of the fiddle and struck and confounded them, and made them give over fiddling and go their way." (Journal I. 231.)

This mighty voice served him well in his open-air preachings, especially amongst the fells of Yorkshire, Westmoreland, and Cumberland, as when from Pardshaw Crag, or the rock above Firbank Chapel, he addressed assembled thousands on the mountain sides.

His bodily strength was great. If it had not been so he would have died in early manhood from the assaults, imprisonments, beatings, fastings, and hardships of every kind which he endured. Similar sufferings terminated the career of most of his young and energetic contemporary preachers; but his powerful frame enabled him to survive all the strains put upon it, and to see the barque of Quakerism brought into a quiet haven before he died. When, on one occasion, an officer determined to make him bow by main force, and ran violently against him to knock him down, George quietly maintained himself erect, his adversary being unable to bend that stalwart form.

If occasion required the exertion, he could outrun most men. Indeed his speed of movement at such times acquired for him the reputation of a wizard. For this and similar reasons, when he was arrested by a company of soldiers in Lancashire, they placed a guard at the chimney-opening, fearing lest George might disappear unexpectedly in that direction!

There are current several portraits of George Fox, of which two are widely published. One of these two represents him as a young man of a dismal and fanatical appearance, and gives the idea of a deluded and half-insane visionary. A copy of this portrait (we believe) was exhibited in the picture-gallery at South Kensington. But it is probably a mere libel on Fox, and there appears to be no foundation for its authenticity. The other, and most usual portrait (see *Frontispiece*), represents him, as his contemporaries describe him to have been, a portly, dignified person, of grave, but pleasing expression, and with very bright eyes. The latter portrait was first published, in a separate form, by Thomas Stackhouse, a Quaker bookseller, of Bell Alley, London, who copied it from a plate in an old volume of the seventeenth century. That plate contained six portraits of eminent Nonconformists, as Baxter, Bunyan, and others. Five of these portraits were known to be faithful likenesses of their subjects, whence there is reason to conclude that the remaining one, that of Fox, is probably also a correct delineation.

His dress was simple, and does not appear to have

differed in cut or style from the usual apparel of sober
men of the period. His grey suit with "alchemy
buttons" is mentioned, also his strong "leather
breeches" for travelling, or for wear in perilous ex-
peditions. His linen was scrupulously clean. When
itinerating on foot he took care to carry a supply of it
with him. On one occasion when brought before a
magistrate (during his first journey to Yorkshire) as
being a suspicious character, the justice exclaimed, "He
is not a vagrant by his linen," and presently liberated
him. A principal source of his trouble during his imprisonments was the intolerably filthy condition of the
gaols. For instance, the state of Carlisle gaol, at the
time of his confinement there, was so horrible that a
woman was almost eaten to death by vermin.

He was very temperate and even abstemious, living for
many weeks at a time on vegetable diet, and frequently
fasting in early life. During his days of special ministry
he sometimes omitted dinner altogether, or merely refreshed himself with a draught of water. In later life
he took a little wine (as mentioned in a letter by Sarah
Fell), but he was always a special advocate of sobriety,
both by precept and example. William Penn speaks of
his "exemplary sobriety" in all respects. His indulgence in sleep was also very limited. He was habitually
an early riser, and repeatedly owed to this practice his
escape from apprehension by magistrates and constables.

He was a man of great shrewdness. He repeatedly
detected flaws in the indictments presented against him
by his persecutors at assizes and sessions. For example,
when arraigned before Judge Turner at Lancaster, he

exposed one discrepancy after another, both as to date and fact, in the indictment, until the local justices "stamped" with rage. At another assize-trial he detected other similar mistakes, which irritated the judge to exclaim, "Take him away, gaoler, take him away." At a third assize-trial (at Launceston) Chief Justice Glyn commanded him to take off his hat. George replied, "Where did ever any magistrate, king, or judge, from Moses to Daniel, command any to put off their hats when they came before them in their courts?—And if the law of England doth command any such thing—show me that law, either written or printed." Then the judge grew very angry, and said, "I do not carry my lawbooks on my back." "But," said George, "tell me where it is printed in any statute-book that I may read it." The judge exclaimed, "Take him away, prevaricator!" George adds, "So they took us away and put us among the thieves." Presently after, he calls to the gaoler, "Bring them up again." When they came in, the judge said to them, "Come, where had they *hats* 'from Moses to Daniel'; come, answer me, I have you fast now." But he did not know his man—George, who was, like Apollos, "mighty in the Scripture," unhesitatingly responded, "Thou mayst read in the third of Daniel, that the three children were cast into the fiery furnace by Nebuchadnezzar's command, with their coats, their hose, and their *hats* on." Once more the baffled and enraged judge cried out, "Take them away, gaoler."

On one occasion, Fox met a man whose finger had just been cut off by an intoxicated person on horseback. The latter having been stopped, George ordered a person to get on the horse and ride on to the nearest magistrate, remarking, "that the offender would be sure to follow lest he should lose his horse." Again, when entering Leicester gaol, George wished to make some arrangements for the comfort of himself and his companions, but first took the precaution of inquiring who was the master there, whether the gaoler or his wife? The latter proved to be the head of authority, for, " although she was lame, and sat mostly in her chair, not being able to go but on crutches, yet she would beat her husband when he came within her reach, if he did not as she would have him." Accordingly, George made his negotiations with the wife. He adds, respecting her husband, " Before we came, when those few Friends that were prisoners there met together (on the Sabbath) if any of them was moved to pray to the Lord, the gaoler would come up with his quarter-staff in his hand, and his mastiff-dog at his heels, and pluck them down by the hair of the head, and strike them with his staff; but when he struck Friends, the mastiff-dog, instead of falling upon Friends, would take the staff out of his hand." (Journal II. 16.)

Whether we should add to the illustrations of George Fox's shrewdness the fact that he systematically avoided taking physic, may be a matter for difference of opinion. But, at any rate, he retained good health to an advanced period of life without having recourse to doctors or medicine. Yet we find that he had a good opinion of the medicinal virtues of herbs for others. In early life he had some thought of becoming a doctor. And at his death he bequeathed a piece of ground in Philadelphia, given him by W. Penn, for the purpose of a botanic garden. This is, perhaps, the first idea of a botanic garden in English history. He also ordered another portion of his Philadelphia land to be devoted to the purpose of a playground for the boys and girls of the city.

William Penn calls him "a divine and a *naturalist*," and adds, "I have been surprised at his questions and answers in natural things." He often refers in particular to the spiritual things of which various plants and animals are types or emblems. In this respect George Fox partially anticipated Swedenborg in the development of the doctrine of "correspondences" between the material and immaterial creation, as interpreted by the science of symbolism.

Thus, in one place he writes, "The Lord showed me that the natures of those things which were hurtful without, were within, in the hearts and minds of wicked men. The natures of dogs, swine, vipers, of Sodom and Egypt, Pharaoh, Cain, Ishmael, Esau, &c. ; the natures of these I saw within, though people had been looking without."

"I saw also how people read the Scriptures without a right sense of them, and without duly applying them to their own states.

"Thus I saw it was an easy matter to say, death reigned from Adam to Moses, &c.; but none could know *how* death reigned from Adam to Moses, &c., but by the same Holy Spirit that Moses was in." The Mosaic types, the journeys of the Israelites, the experiences of the Jews under Judges and Kings, the construction of the Tabernacle and Temple, were all to be studied in the light of Christ and by His Spirit. He adds : "As man comes through, by the Spirit and power of God, to Christ, who fulfils the

types, figures, shadows, promises and prophecies that were
of Him, and is led by the Holy Ghost into *the truth
and substance* of the Scriptures, sitting down in Him who
is the author and end of them, then are they read and
understood with profit and great delight."

From inattention to this principle of study, the Bible is
so often a " dry" book even to professing Christians.

His judgment (at any rate after his early experiences)
was good, and commanded the respect and deference of his
coadjutors. William Penn further records of him: "Though
God had visibly clothed him with a divine preference and
authority, yet he never abused it, but held his place in the
church of God with great meekness and a most engaging
humility and moderation. By night and by day, by sea
and by land, in this and in foreign countries, I never saw
him out of his place, or not a match for every service
or occasion." Another of his contemporaries, speaking of
his presence at the deliberations of the principal Friends,
remarked, " I observe that when George is present, the
others are mostly silent." Again, in the old records
of the London Friends we find that, at the appointment
of committees to manage various matters, the entry is
sometimes made respecting the most difficult questions,
" We will leave this for G. F."

We have already alluded to his courage. It was indomitable. Wherever there was special peril George
would present himself, not in rashness, but as the leader
of his people, and that he might bear the brunt of the
battle. Thus, when the sudden and fanatic outbreak of
the Fifth Monarchy Men occurred in London, about
1660, when the passions of the mob were especially

excited against the Friends, who were believed (without any reason) to be connected with that mad movement, George Fox boldly walked the streets as usual, and sought opportunities of publicly showing himself, at the risk of his life, as a peaceable and orderly citizen. Again, whenever magistrates and constables threatened to come and break up particular gatherings of the Friends, if he happened to be anywhere in the neighbourhood, he took care to present himself at the post of danger, both to confront his adversaries and to assist his brethren. He was haled before magistrates sixty times in thirty-six years.

Like his wife, George was of a kindly cheerful disposition. He records of a very painful illness, " Yet I was pretty cheery, and my spirit kept above it all." This was a constant characteristic. Penn says he was " even in his spirit to the last, as if death were hardly worth notice or a mention," and that he was through life " *neither touchy nor critical.*"

His energy and life-long perseverance were marvellous. These characteristics we have already alluded to. Penn styles him " an incessant labourer." He exercised a constant and simultaneous care over all the companies of his people—from Germany to Virginia. Penn adds : " He was often where the records of the affairs of the church are kept, and the letters from the many meetings of God's people over all the world he had read to him and communicated them to the meeting that is weekly held there [in London] for such services." His correspondence was immense.

We have taken the trouble to count the visits to various localities recorded in his journals. They amount to *up-*

wards of thirteen hundred. Some of these visits occupied months, or even years. They include his travels on both sides of the Atlantic.

For matters requiring scholastic learning and research, his own education had not qualified him; but in these things he had the faculty of availing himself of the attainments of those who (like Penn and Barclay) had received a collegiate training. He was skilful in suggesting the services of such. For instance, when the legality of Quaker marriages was first contested, George Fox promptly wrote to one of his learned friends as follows:

"Now, dear R. R.—I desire that thou would search all the libraries concerning marriages and what they say of them, and the Fathers, and how they did before the Monks first came in; and search histories and laws, and see what thou canst bring out, both good and bad; and what maketh a marriage; and do what thou canst in this thing," &c. (MS. quoted in W. Tanner's "Three Lectures.")

One of his most prominent characteristics was his prayerful vigilance of life and conversation, and his avoidance of "idle words." This conspicuous trait was an indispensable accompaniment of one who sought to be eminently used of the Holy Spirit. In this sobriety of soul, a ministerial qualification so repeatedly urged by the Apostle Paul, (especially in the Epistles to Titus and Timothy,) George Fox, his contemporaries and successors in the ministry, have, for the most part, been very exemplary. One can conceive of no character more inappropriate to a preacher than that of being conspicuous as a jester. Seldom have Friends figured as such. On

this subject an eminent Wesleyan (Rev. Wm. Arthur, in
his "Tongue of Fire," p. 317) thus writes:

"Among the hindrances which will prevent any one
from having the 'tongue of fire,' none acts more directly
than any misuse of the tongue itself. If the door of the
lips be not guarded; if uncharitable or idle speech be
indulged; if political or party discussion be permitted
to excite heats; if 'foolish talking or jesting' be a
chosen method of display, it is not to be supposed that
the same tongue will be a medium wherein the sacred fire
of the Spirit will delight to dwell. Who has ever worn
at the same time the reputation of a trifler and of a man
powerful to search consciences?"

The writer, at a recent religious anniversary at Exeter
Hall, had the pleasure of listening to a forcible and
dignified, yet cheerful, address by the author of the above
quotation. That address and one or two others stood out
in marked and very favourable contrast, as compared with
two speeches at the same meeting, delivered by ministerial
jesters. The absurd anecdotes (several of them of gross
impropriety) and the unctuous flattery of the chairman
indulged in by these gentlemen, although they elicited
the laughter of the younger portion of the assembly,
caused evident sorrow to elder and thoughtful hearers.
Similar exhibitions on the part of some "popular"
ministers are but too frequent. But, happily, the
great body of ministers of all denominations exercise
much care in this respect, yet none more so than the
followers of Fox. These also avoid, in general, the
opposite extreme of sanctimoniousness and the affectation
of gravity by a mere empty dumbness and stolid silence.

The latter weakness used to be a failing of some of the Friends in the last century; but has, in great degree, now disappeared.

George Fox was so thoroughly conversant with the Bible, that the historian Gerard Croese remarks of him: "Having incessantly continued in the study of the Scripture from his infancy to his latter end, he became so exactly versed in them that there was no remarkable saying in all the Holy Writings that escaped his knowledge or remembrance. I have heard some of his friends say, and not those of the vulgar sort, but men of learning and knowledge, that though the Bible were lost it might be found in the mouth of George Fox."

In his autobiographical "Journal" alone, he quotes from upwards of 240 chapters of the Bible. His letters and "Doctrinals" abound everywhere with similar quotations.

The preaching of George Fox was not characterised by eloquence (like that of Edward Burrough or James Naylor); but nevertheless possessed remarkable power. It carried with it "the demonstration of the Spirit." William Penn, in describing it, whilst admitting that his mode of expression was sometimes "uncouth and unfashionable to nice ears," adds that "his matter was nevertheless very profound, and would not only bear to be often considered; but the more it was so, the more weighty and instructing it appeared. God sent him. No arts or parts had any share in the matter or manner of his ministry. He much laboured to open truth to the people's understandings, and to ground them upon the principle and principal, Christ Jesus, the light of the world; that by bringing

them to *something that was of God in themselves*, they
might the better know and judge of Him and themselves.
He had an extraordinary gift in opening the Scriptures.
He would go to the marrow of things."

Penn, in holding up George Fox's example to other
ministers, urges upon such that it is not enough merely to
preach the Gospel verbally. He adds : " But as was the
practice of this man of God, in great measure, when
among us, inquire the state of the several churches you
visit; who among them are afflicted or sick; who are
tempted; and if any are unfaithful or obstinate; and
endeavour to issue those things, in the wisdom and
power of God, which will be a glorious crown upon your
ministry."

CHAPTER IX.

FOX'S ADDITIONS TO THE BAPTIST SYSTEM—THE QUAKER POLITY.

RECAPITULATION OF THE BAPTIST INSTITUTES ADOPTED BY FOX—THE QUAKER CODE OF DISCIPLINE—PRACTICAL RESTRICTIONS OF THE MINISTRY—ALBERT FOX AND JOSEPH STEPHENS — VALUE OF MINISTERIAL BREVITY — FEMALE PREACHERS—FOX'S UNIVERSAL PHILANTHROPY—HIS PLEA FOR SLAVES AND INDIANS—HIS LABOURS FOR EDUCATION —HIS SYMPATHY FOR THE POOR AND FOR DOMESTIC SERVANTS — INCULCATION OF TEMPERANCE — HIS VIEWS RESPECTING THE PENAL CODE, THE MAGISTRACY, AND CIVIL GOVERNMENT—HIS WISE COUNSELS AS THE QUAKER LEADER.

As we have already seen, the ecclesiastical system of Quakerism, both as to doctrine and discipline, had been in most respects anticipated by the General Baptists. Many details and subsequent modifications were, however, added by Fox, who rendered it a much more clearly defined and permanently settled polity than the Baptists had ever possessed. Besides the omission of the two visible ordinances, he also discontinued several other Baptist or Puritan institutes, and added two special contributions, which we shall presently refer to. But, after allowing for all changes, the resemblance between the organisations of the two sects is most striking, both in general aspect and minute particulars. As so many of these have been considered in a former chapter, we will merely recapitulate the features of the General Baptist system held in common with the Friends, viz. :

1. The regular holding of monthly, quarterly, and annual or general "meetings for discipline," and the appointment of "representatives" from the former to the latter.

2. A careful system of inquiries or "queries" respecting the conduct of all the members, the doctrine of ministers, and the attendance of meetings for worship; also, a system of prompt dealing with delinquents.

3. Liberal and systematic maintenance of all the poorer members.

4. A preference for small congregations as organised churches of the body.

5. Recognition of the priesthood of believers as "a society of equals," with liberty of preaching for all, and the public congregational acknowledgment of approved speakers.

6. Disapproval (at first) of instrumental music, and discouragement of singing, except by persons whose experiences qualified them to use the words of psalms and hymns.

7. A mode of marriage much resembling that of the Friends.

8. Disciplinary treatment of persons "marrying out" of the sect.

9. Disuse of the heathen names of months and days.

10. Disuse (by some of the early Baptists) of the pronoun "you" to single persons.

11. Rejection of infant baptism.

12. Special testimonies against "superfluity of apparel," &c.

13. Scruples against oaths and tithes.

14. Objection of many Baptists to war also.

15. Objection (at first) to payment of ministers.

16. Repudiation of learning and collegiate training as essentials for ministers.

17. Recognition of spiritual gifts, for the service of the church, in women.

18. Objection to terms "Trinity," "Sacrament," &c.

19. Recognition of the continuance of inward revelations from God.

20. Denial of the authority of the civil power in matters of conscience.

Only a portion of these have been maintained by the modern Baptists.

Whilst George Fox improved upon the Baptist system in some respects, he failed to imitate its thoroughly scriptural simplicity in one or-.two other important matters; and hence schism and unsoundness have subsequently been experienced by his Society, until modern Quakerism has, by sheer force of necessity, been compelled to supply his omissions.

The Baptist historian, speaking of the discipline of the early members of his body, says, " Nor did they, like the Presbyterians, who profess to condemn prescribed models, publish a long directory, to instruct the administrator in the due mode of discharging every part of his duty. No; they left their ministers and brethren to study that infallible directory, the Word of God, and to regulate their procedure in all affairs of a religious nature, to the best of their own judgments, in conformity to that sacred standard. Happy would it have been for the cause of truth had all Christians acted on the same principles."

Yet some of the disciplinary practices of the Friends in Fox's days were more simple and untrammelled than those of his modern representatives. For instance, the exercise of ministry was more really free to every individual who believed it his duty to preach than in the subsequent periods of Quakerism. The early Friends had no distinct order of ministers. They testified against clerical orders of *every* kind. They permitted any of their members to travel as preachers without the formal, and often very *irregular*, restraints of modern Quakerism.

After the establishment of the Society there arose a custom of giving certificates of approval to travelling ministers ; but these documents were not made the essential and restrictive instruments that they have been rendered in later times. Now-a-days Friends do not practically enjoy liberty of ministry until they are formally "acknowledged" as such by their "Monthly Meetings." And if they travel as preachers without having such "acknowledgment," or without a "certificate," they are regarded virtually as transgressors. This is wholly inconsistent with Foxian Quakerism, which permitted and encouraged a fulness of freedom in preaching not recognised by the practice of the modern Friends. Again, the "acknowledged" ministers now form a distinct body having special privileges and pre-eminence. And yet a large proportion of the most edifying and scriptural ministry in the Society is exercised by members who are never "acknowledged."

The principle of Fox and his contemporaries was that the appointment and call of ministers appertained to God only, and that merely their recognition belongs to the church. The modern Friends admit this in theory, but often deny it in practice. They sometimes virtually impose restraints neither scriptural nor Friendly on their members, and, in practice, say, " Although you may be called of God to the work of the ministry, and although, further, your conduct may be quite as becoming as that of the officially " acknowledged " minister, yet, if you happen to be in any respect the object of local or influential criticism, we shall not recognise your church services, and we shall place obstacles in the exercise of your apprehended duty to preach the Gospel."

To adduce living instances of this exclusiveness would be invidious ; but, for the sake of proof, some very recent cases must be alluded to. For example, there died, in 1867, a very pious and philanthropic Friend named Albert Fox, whose biography has just been published under the title of the " Devout Merchant " (by Rev. John Jones, of Liverpool). For many years this good man preached at the Quaker meetings of London and Liverpool ; the excellence of his doctrine and the holiness of his life were beyond question. Meanwhile, minister after minister was " acknowledged," with qualifications for gospel service in no wise superior, if indeed equal, to those of this devoted man, and still he remained under the disadvantage of implied disapproval, and received, both directly and indirectly, frequent discouragement. There was no reason whatever for this, except that he cared less for mere Quaker routine than for scriptural simplicity. As soon as he was dead the Friends widely and warmly acknowledged his virtues.

Again, there died recently, at Thornbury, near Bristol, a pious Friend, in humble life, named Joseph Stephens. He had been from childhood a genuine Christian. He was in request for miles around his dwelling as a visitor to the sick and dying, of other denominations. His sermons, though expressed in homely and often ungrammatical language, possessed more fervour and life than those of at least three-fourths of the addresses of " acknowledged " Quaker ministers. Joseph Stephens died as he had lived—a peculiarly exemplary Christian, but he, too, was never " acknowledged " ; but, on the contrary, repeatedly received the express discouragement of the Society. Like good Albert Fox, he was simply scriptural, not traditional. We need not give further instances of this kind, but very many similar ones might be adduced.

Theoretically, the Friends recognise " the priesthood of all believers," and protest against a ministerial order ; but their practice is often and markedly inconsistent with their theory in both respects. Many of the Friends are now admitting this. One of their most influential members, residing at Tottenham, has recently refused to permit his name to be enrolled amongst the "acknowledged " ministers, though pressed to allow it by the congregation, because he perceives the inconsistency of the practice of modern Quakerism with the rules and doctrines of its first leaders. George Fox freely encouraged the exercise of preaching by conscientious persons, who believed it to be their call and duty. He was very careful not to "quench the spirit" in any.

At the same time he repeatedly recommended *order* in the churches. This watchword is needed in modern Quakerism, mainly by some who are apt to preach at too great length and on many various topics at the same time. At the meetings for worship during the Quarterly and Yearly assemblies of the modern Friends, it is a common thing for *nearly all* the time to be occupied by preachers, whose utterances are sometimes of the most promiscuous and unconnected nature. The old scriptural rule of "let the prophets speak, *two or three*," might be often remembered with advantage. Single sermons, embracing half a dozen unassociated topics, followed by other sermons as promiscuous, often characterise such gatherings. Quaker ministers are sometimes apt to regard what they term "the relief of their own minds" more than the edification of their audience in these gatherings. It needs to be ever remembered that worship—prayer and adoration—and *not* exhortation or preaching should be the *chief* object and exercise of every such religious gathering. It is written, "My house shall be called a house of prayer."

In the disproportionate amount of preaching, as compared with prayerful meditation, the Friends' meetings in America are far more open to objection than those in Great Britain. A Quaker lady—herself a preacher—stated on her return from the United States, that the Friends' spiritual life was almost "preached to death" in the West. Another English Friend, after an American journey in 1867, has described some of the meetings of the Society in Indiana as being so slightly characterised

by silence, that the constant succession of speakers
conveys the impression of wide-spread morbid impulses
to utterance. Thus at a protracted Quakers' "meeting
for worship" in Indiana in 1867, *ninety* Friends preached
and prayed. Some of the American lady speakers appear
to be the most fluent and full—delivering addresses of
from sixty to ninety minutes' duration. Such discourses,
in addition to others, produce a sensation for which
repletion is a mild term.

It must be confessed, that in England also the lengthi-
ness and promiscuousness of discourse is chiefly indulged
in by some of the sister ministers.

George Fox, and the early Baptists before him, rightly
recognised the importance of the exercise of spiritual
gifts by women. Both the Old and New Testament
recognise the gift of ministry to these; but they explicitly
limit the *place* of its exercise. Paul says : "I suffer not
a woman to speak *in the churches.* There was no female
apostle, nor any female missionary sent forth by our
Saviour or by the Apostles as a *public* preacher. But
doubtless many good women were qualified by the Holy
Ghost to minister edification and consolation in the more
private circles of the church, and by household visitation
or family influence. The Friends (including George Fox)
appear to have greatly overlooked this scriptural *limitation*
of women's ministry. They have rightly permitted it a
place in the church, but have often suffered from giving
it too great liberty, beyond the biblical examples and
rules respecting it.

The two special features for which Quakerism is somewhat distinctly indebted to George Fox are, first, his

peculiar enforcement of the *perceptibility* of the individual-ising communications or impressions afforded by the presence of the Holy Spirit in the hearts of believers; secondly, the consequent practice of worshipping to a considerable extent in silence, in order to facilitate the clear perception of these spiritual impressions.

This free and perceptible access of the Holy Spirit to the members of the church, of course also involves the individual responsibility to God so often and specially urged and claimed by the Friends.

But even these two special features of Quakerism were not wholly original to Fox. We find many traces of them in the preceding and contemporaneous history, both of the pious Mystics (on the continent and in England) and also in the customs of the Puritans and Baptists in their small gatherings for solemn worship and Christian communion.

George Fox *extended and intensified* the Baptist system in many departments of a philanthropic nature, and thereby promoted the expansion and activity of the Quaker mind. Many of the distinguishing, benevolent movements of subsequent Quakerism were thus antici-pated, in actual effort or in suggestion, by him.

Thus, respecting the *Slavery of Africans*, one of the highest authorities—Thomas Clarkson—has written in his "Portraiture of Quakerism," that "George Fox was probably the first person who publicly declared against this species of slavery; for *nothing that could be deplored by humanity seems to have escaped his eye.*"

When in 1671 he visited Barbadoes, he advised his friends there "to endeavour to train up their negroes in

the fear of God, that so, with Joshua, every member of a
family might say, 'As for me and my house, we will
serve the Lord.' " He adds : "I desired also that they
would cause their overseers to deal mildly and gently with
their negroes, and not use cruelty toward them; and that
after certain years of servitude they should make them
free; and when they go and are made free, let them not
go away empty-handed." In 1679 he wrote to the
American Friends : "All Friends everywhere that have
Indians or blacks, you are to preach the Gospel to them,
and other servants, if you be true Christians."

For the promotion of *Education* George Fox laboured
assiduously. In this respect he far surpassed the Baptists,
and added a great improvement to the discipline adapted
from them. He procured the establishment both of
boarding and day schools in connection with the Metropolitan and other meetings of the Society. He desired
that the education given in these schools should be a
liberal and comprehensive one, embracing, to use his own
expression, "all things civil and useful in the creation."
He wrote to Friends in 1779 : "Now, you, having your
food from Christ, and God your Father, cannot you train
up your children in the fear of God, and tell them from
whence you have your good things, that they may come
to receive of all these good things from the good God and
Christ, the treasure of wisdom and knowledge?" He
also exhorted in an address issued in 1683 : "It is desired
that all Friends that have children, families and servants,
may train them up in the pure and unspotted religion,
and in the nurture and fear of God; *and that frequently
they read the Holy Scriptures, and exhort and admonish*

them that every family apart may serve and worship the Lord, as well as in public." On another occasion he wrote : " Now, dear Friends, consider old Eli's case, who did admonish his children ; but because he did not *restrain* them from the follies and the evils they ran into, therefore the Lord brought his judgments upon him." Quakerism in its subsequent course owes much of its influence and excellence to Fox's educational zeal. That zeal was the more remarkable in a man who had himself enjoyed very few and scanty privileges in this direction.

His inculcation of *practical Sympathy for the Poor* was constant and effectual. In all the meetings of Friends he secured a systematic attention to the necessities of the poor, especially of orphans and " desolate widows." He recommended almshouses for " poor Friends that are past work," also the establishment of a large institution " where one hundred may have rooms to work in, and shops of all sorts of things to sell, and where widows and young women might work and live." He exhorted the well-to-do amongst his brethren to entertain the poor at their social gatherings, reminding them that " he that giveth to the poor lendeth to the Lord ;" and that although " they cannot recompense thee, yet thou shalt be recompensed at the resurrection of the just." He adds : " So you will have the blessings of the Lord and the blessings of the poor ; and so be of a free noble spirit, above all the churlish misers and niggards and narrow spirits."

He enforces the principle that over-anxiety to save money at the expense of charity is a practical *distrust of the Lord's future care*, and a faithless disloyalty to Christ.

The kindly consideration of the position and claims of *Domestic Servants* was another branch of Christian charity which he did not overlook in his exhortations. His followers have, in general, given much attention to this important subject, and it is made one of the matters of periodical inquiry amongst Friends.

If other Christian denominations had been as careful in this respect, an incalculable amount of vice and crime would have been prevented. Doubtless, at the great Day of Judgment, many highly professing persons who, as mistresses of servants and masters of apprentices, have needlessly exposed their dependants to temptation, and have neglected to extend a protecting care to their weakness, will be made awfully responsible for much of the robbery, prostitution, and ruin which have necessarily resulted. How many poor youths and girls have been turned adrift, penniless and unshielded, to become the certain prey of the spoiler, by employers holding a high position in the reputation even of the churches. But the final and abiding decision on this and in innumerable other matters may be diametrically opposed to that of the canons of " respectability" and " right" recognised by many of our merely human and social verdicts.

Although living two centuries before the days of *Teetotalism*, George Fox, viewing with sorrow the evils of intemperance, vigorously protested against placing temptations to this vice in the way of any, whether old or young. In 1682, he issued an earnest address on this subject to vintners and innkeepers, exhorting them not to " destroy them that have not power over their lusts. For, when they are overcome by strong liquors, then are they fit for all manner of wickedness." He adds: "And though you think, by selling or letting people have wine or strong liquors more than doth them good, or is for their health, that the more they drink the more gain it brings you—ah, poor sellers! do not you think that God with His all-seeing eye doth behold you and your actions? God will destroy them who destroy the earth."

The *Treatment of Criminals and the Condition of Prison Discipline* were not likely to escape George Fox's attention amid his repeated incarcerations. During one of his imprisonments he wrote to the judges protesting against capital punishment, and exhorting the rulers to "show mercy, that you may receive mercy from God the Judge of all." He says: "Moreover, I laid before the judges what an hurtful thing it was that prisoners should lie so long in gaol; showing how they learned wickedness one of another in talking of their bad deeds, and therefore speedy justice should be done." He advocated the adoption of the Mosaic plan of compelling thieves to make restitution to those they had injured.

The Friends have always been prominent in efforts for the abolition of capital punishment and for the amelioration of prison discipline. During Fox's lifetime his friend William Penn, in founding the laws and administration of Pennsylvania, established a system of penal treatment which was then, and still remains, after the lapse of nearly two centuries, unsurpassed for its combination of humanity, wisdom and practical efficiency. But neither Fox nor Penn advocated any impunity to crime. When some of the early Friends expressed scruples against serving as constables and watchmen, and thereby associating themselves with the powers of the State for the forcible repression of crime, George Fox issued an address containing the following remonstrance: "If any should come to burn your house or rob you, or come to assault your wives or daughters; or a company should come to fire a city or town, or come to kill people, won't you watch against such evil things, in the power of God in your own way? You cannot but discover such things to the magistrates who are to punish such things; and therefore the watch is kept and set to discover such to the magistrate that they may be punished; and if he does it not, he bears his sword in vain. And for this cause we pay tribute."

George Fox believed that *war* was *incompatible with Christianity*, or at any rate with the advanced stages of it. When his friend Penn asked him if he might continue to wear a sword, he replied, "Wear it as long as thou canst;" thereby implying his assurance that Penn would feel such a practice to be inconsistent with a decidedly serious life. Some of Fox's coadjutors do not appear to have altogether disapproved of war. Thus his right-hand ally, the fervent Edward Burrough, exhorted a troop of soldiers to fidelity and obedience, telling them that "perhaps the Lord might have a work for them to do in fighting against the Pope." The early Friends also recognised Cromwell as an instrument of good until he yielded to the sectarian bigots who induced him to become a persecutor.

George Fox's Christian wisdom as the chief leader of the Friends is well illustrated by one of his pastoral letters, respecting the management of the Society's Meetings for Discipline. It is dated March, 1690 (the year in which he died), and is a document containing counsel well worthy of the attention of church-gatherings of every denomination.

"Let all your meetings be preserved by the wisdom of God, in the unity of the Spirit, the bond of peace, and the fellowship of the Holy Ghost, that, being ordered by the pure, gentle, heavenly, peaceable wisdom, easy to be entreated, they may be holy and virtuous examples to all other meetings, both in city and country.

"Let all be careful to speak shortly and pertinently to matters, in a Christian spirit, and dispatch business quickly, and keep out of long debates and heats; and, with the Spirit of God, keep that down which is doating about questions and strifes of words, that tend to parties and contention. In the church of God there is no such custom to be allowed.

"And let not more than one speak at a time; nor any in a fierce way; for that is not to be allowed in any society, either natural or spiritual. But as the Apostle saith, 'Be swift to hear and slow to speak;' and let it be in the grace which seasons all words.

"And if there be any differences that cannot be quickly ended in the meeting, order some Friends to hear the matter out of the meeting without respect of persons, and bring in the report to the same meeting, the same day if possible, and the meeting may give judgment, that no business be delayed from time to time.

"And so my love to you all, in the seed of life, Christ Jesus, in whom ye have all peace and wisdom, from Him who is the treasure of knowledge and wisdom."

All the philanthropic or theological additions made by

Fox to the polity and character of the discipline and doctrine found by him among the early General Baptists, originated mainly in *the one special* addition which he imported into the Quaker-Baptist system, viz. his intense inculcation of religious *individualism*. By this term we mean the deeper sense of individual private responsibility to the Divine Father and King of all, and the more profound, more practical, more defined inculcation of the access of each Christian to the perceptible influence and guidance of the Holy Spirit in his own heart, as his own Divine oracle, and as his centre of responsibility and authority.

This principle of the *perceptibility* of the *individualising* visitations of the Holy Spirit constitutes, especially in connection with its encouragement of the practice of *silent worship*, the root and essence of Quakerism as a *particular* branch of the Church Catholic and Apostolic. But it requires to be ever associated with the collateral and harmonious authority of Holy Scripture as a test, and as an accompanying blessing of richly additional efficacy. This accompaniment (too often insufficiently urged) is of the utmost importance. It is essential, not merely as an accompaniment, but as a *producing* and *developing cause* of spiritual influences.

The diligent prayerful use of Holy Scripture is, in great degree at least, the very organ and chief channel of the Holy Spirit. *This* is also the main and unbroken "channel of *apostolical succession*," both to churches and individual Christians.

CHAPTER X.

LAST DAYS AND DECEASE.

THE DECLINE OF LIFE—FOX WITNESSES THE CESSATION OF
STUART PERSECUTION—HIS DILIGENCE IN OLD AGE—EN-
COUNTERS SOME OPPOSITION FROM HIS FRIENDS AT TIMES
—PRESENTS A MEETING-HOUSE TO THE SOCIETY—ATTENDS
THE YEARLY MEETING OF 1690—LABOURS TO THE LAST—
DIES IN PEACE—HIS FUNERAL—RE-INTERMENT—HIS SUPE-
RIORITY TO ALL HIS COLLEAGUES—HIS GROWTH IN GRACE
AND IN HUMILITY—TRUTH IS MANY-SIDED—HENCE THE
ESSENTIAL FUNCTION OF SECTS—THE HARMONIOUS VARIETY
OF TRUTH—THE MISSION OF MODERN QUAKERISM.

THE latter years of George Fox's life were spent chiefly
in the neighbourhood of London, or at Swarthmoor Hall,
or in comparatively quiet journeys through some of the
counties. During this period, he received the honour
and affectionate esteem of faithful adherents, wherever he
went; for the Society was now well established throughout the kingdom. Hence the evening of life was
soothed with the sunshine of many precious friendships.
Further, a relaxation of the severe penal laws against
Dissenters, followed on the death of Charles the Second,
and during the reign of James the Second. William
Penn was high in favour at court, and enjoyed the per-

sonal friendship of the king and of his chief officers of
state. Hence the Friends obtained much toleration.
Then came the peaceful but effectual Revolution which
resulted in the accession of William of Orange and the
permanent cessation of the miseries and persecutions
which, under two centuries of Tudor and Stuart rule, had
distracted Great Britain, and involved her best and
noblest sons in almost ceaseless struggles for the rights
of conscience—struggles during which so many tens of
thousands had, in one way or another, resisted unto
martyrdom. George Fox lived to welcome the dawning
of these peaceful and sunny years, and having witnessed
this end of strife, he passed, with the calm assurance of
mature faith, into the invisible realities of that kingdom
where no sorrow or wrong is permitted to cloud the
everlasting brightness of its celestial joys.

To the last he maintained an affectionate superin-
tendence over the numerous home and foreign churches,
established through the instrumentality of himself and
his colleagues. He gave constant attention to the over-
sight of the records and registers of the Society, and
personally maintained a vast correspondence. In these
works he was greatly aided by Ellis Hookes, the first
" recording clerk " of the Society of Friends.

During these latter years of his life, George Fox com-
pleted his journals and theological works, and arranged
and endorsed the large accumulation of letters and
manuscripts now in the possession of the Society of
Friends, and in that of the various descendants of the
Fell family.

The unintermitting industry of his last days was

maintained amid great and increasing infirmities. Even his naturally powerful frame was now slowly but surely yielding to the inevitable laws of mortality. Thus, between 1680 and 1690, he repeatedly records such entries as the following : " When I had stayed about a month in London, I got out of town again; for by reason of the many hardships I had undergone in imprisonments and other sufferings for Truth's sake, my body was grown so infirm and weak that I could not bear the closeness of the city long together ; but was fain to go a little into the country, where I might have the benefit of the fresh air. At this time I went with my son-in-law, William Mead, to his country house called Gooseyes, in Essex (near Barking), where I stayed about two weeks." In this manner he frequently visited his friends and relatives at Gooseyes, Kingston, Winchmoor Hill, Tottenham, Edmonton, Waltham, Shacklewell, and other suburban spots. But even during these periods of weakness and relaxation, he often mentions having " good service " in holding or attending meetings, in visiting the poor and sick, and in other branches of Christian service. Still abiding in the eternal Vine, the Lord Jesus, he could not but be fruitful even in the most advanced hours of life.

A year before his decease he writes: " About the middle of the First Month, 1689, I went to London, the Parliament then sitting, and being then about the Bill·for Indulgence. Though I was weak in body and not well able to stir to and fro, yet so great a concern was upon my spirit on behalf of Truth and Friends, that I attended continually for many days with other Friends, at the

N

Parliament house, labouring with the members thereof
that the thing might be done comprehensively and effectually." The term "Truth" was frequently used by the
early Friends to signify the Christian religion in its
thorough, inward, and unconventional simplicity. We
find the same peculiar expression in use among the early
Baptists. Thus, John Matthews, who is mentioned in
1647 as "a teacher in the church" of the General Baptists, was thus described by his friend Denne (also a
Baptist): "He not only owned the Truth, but likewise
preached it publicly to the world; at which time the
Spirit and power of God was so manifested in him,
that none of the adversaries durst open their mouths to
oppose it."

The course of George Fox's declining years was not
wholly smooth, for there arose, even amongst his first
followers, some who opposed the disciplinary or other
institutes adopted by him. Many of his pastoral epistles
were issued to reprove or answer such dissentients. Some
of the latter were probably not always in the wrong,
especially when objecting to needless formalisms which
were already creeping into the young church of Quakerism.
Thus, one John Perrott was severely censured, if not
formally excommunicated, because he chose to assert his
individual liberty by wearing a beard, a custom which,
from some old Puritan and Roundhead prejudices against
the Cavaliers, appears to have been generally deemed
inadmissible by the first Friends. Even George Fox himself was often criticised for allowing his hair to grow long.
He was more liberal than many of his contemporaries and
successors in the Society, and persisted in the obnoxious

habit simply as a protest against bigoted and unscriptural assumptions.

Two other Quaker dissentients of the period were Wilkinson and Story, who had sharply criticised the "singings and soundings" of the early Friends in their meetings. In those days the use of hymns and praises (as amongst the Baptists and other sects) was still retained in some Quaker meetings. (Janney's "Life of Fox," p. 360.)

Serious charges against the theology of the Society were brought forward by George Keith and several others. (Keith was a prominent Quaker preacher, who eventually became a clergyman in the Church of England, and was the first foreign missionary appointed by the then recently formed "Society for the Propagation of the Gospel," that grand old association which, though not without some weak points, has sent out so many earnest Christian ministers to evangelise the remotest regions of the earth.) These charges were mainly directed against defective views respecting the Trinity, the Atonement, and against the extravagant procedure of some of the Quaker female preachers. It has been the uniform custom of Quaker writers to represent Keith, and other dissentients, as being altogether in the wrong; but those who, in an impartial and unsectarian spirit, desire to "hear both sides," will easily perceive that George Fox and his followers did really and not unfrequently lay themselves fairly open to the criticism of other good Christians.

The condition of English Quakerism until the end of the eighteenth century, and in America till far on in the nineteenth century, was sometimes almost such as was

indicated by a Friend from the United States, who
thus described transatlantic Quakerism as it existed
previous to the Hicksite schism: "We did not hear
anything about Jesus of Nazareth in our meetings
before William Forster came over (in 1820); the difference between you and us is just this—you believe in
an outward Saviour, we believe in a Saviour within."
(Letter quoted by William Ball in *The Friend* news-
paper, January 1, 1868.) This description is, however,
an exaggerated one.

Before George Fox died he executed a deed of assign-
ment, conveying to the Friends, for ever, a house and
several acres of land near Swarthmoor, for the purpose
and maintenance of a meeting-house. He says: "It is
all the land and house I have in England; and it is given
up to the Lord, for it is for His service and for His
children." He also caused a Bible to be chained to a
desk in the meeting for reference. He sometimes
preached with a Bible in his hand, hence it is evident
that he did not practically claim the exaggerated "inspiration" which some of his successors of extreme views were
accustomed, till late years, to plead for, viz. an inspiration
independent of the aids of memory and biblical research.

In April, 1690, George Fox attended, for the last time,
the annual gathering of Friends from all parts of the
kingdom, held in London. In describing that meeting he
says: "Many useful and necessary things relating to the
safety of Friends and to the honour and prosperity of
Truth were weightily treated of and unanimously concluded."

The summer and autumn of that year witnessed the last

labours of this very earnest man. In September he issued
a final appeal to his fellow preachers, exhorting—" Not
to cumber yourselves nor entangle yourselves with the
affairs of this world. For the natural soldiers are not to
cumber themselves with the world, much less the soldiers
of Christ, who are not of this world, but are to mind the
riches and glory of the world that is everlasting. Do not
sit down, Demas-like, and embrace this present world
that will have an end, lest ye become idolaters. As able
ministers of the Spirit sow to the Spirit, that of the Spirit
ye may reap life everlasting. All you that preach the truth,
do it *as it is in Jesus, in love.* For all that be in Christ
are in love, peace, and unity."

Throughout October and November he continued to
attend meetings almost daily. On the 10th of November,
having heard that the Friends in Ireland were undergoing
troubles and trials, he wrote them an affectionate pastoral
letter, exhorting them to turn to " His supporting hand
and power, who is God, all-sufficient to strengthen, help,
and refresh in time of need. Let none forget the Lord's
mercies and kindnesses which endure for ever ; but always
live in the sense of them." He concludes with the words,
—" So all of you live and walk in Christ Jesus ; that
nothing may be between you and God, but Christ, in
whom ye have salvation, life, rest, and peace with God."

He then added this postscript, indicating " the universal
spirit " which, as Penn justly remarks, characterised him
to the last : " As for the affairs of Truth, in this land and
abroad, I hear that in Holland and Germany, and there-
away, Friends are in love, unity, and peace ; and in
Jamaica, Barbadoes, Nevis, Antigua, Maryland, and New

England, I hear nothing but Friends are in unity and
peace. The Lord preserve them all out of the world, in
which there is trouble, in Christ Jesus, in whom there is
peace, life, love, and unity.—Amen. My love in the Lord
Jesus Christ to all Friends everywhere in your land, as
though I named them."

After writing these words of affection and heartfelt
piety he laid down the pen for ever. The next day, being
the Sabbath, he attended a large meeting of Friends at
Gracechurch Street, where he preached for the last time
"fully and effectually." Presently afterward he knelt in
solemn prayer. When the meeting ended he went into
the house of a Friend close by, in White Hart Court, and
remarked that he thought " he felt the cold strike to his
heart as he came out of the meeting." But he added, " I
am glad I was here ; *now I am clear ; I am fully clear.*"
He at once lay down, and soon becoming worse, retired to
bed, where, says Penn, " he lay in much contentment and
peace, and very sensible to the last."

On the Monday and Tuesday many Friends visited
him, and, although dying, the departing saint appeared
absorbed in " his interest for the welfare of the churches,
and in conversation on the promotion of the Gospel. He
sent many parting messages of love and counsel to his
beloved companions far and near. The Irish and
American communities of his brethren were specially remembered by him as being distant from the care of the
prominent English leaders of the Society. Twice did the
dying elder (a true bishop in the New Testament sense of
the word) exclaim to his faithful coadjutors assembled
round his bedside : " Mind poor Friends in Ireland and

America!" Amongst his last words were: "All is well —I am weak in body, yet never heed; the power of God is over all."

His last hours were free from any sign of pain. On Tuesday evening, he calmly closed his eyes with his own hands, and, in perfect repose and peace, fell asleep in the Lord. The chin never fell, nor needed binding up. William Penn wrote of him, in death: "One would have thought he smiled. He was the most pleasant corpse that I ever looked upon."

On the following Friday the funeral took place. After a solemn meeting for worship, of two hours' duration, the procession of 3,000 Friends walked in rows of three abreast, from Lombard Street to the Quaker burial-ground at Finsbury. Each of the Metropolitan Meetings had appointed six Friends to assist in carrying the body of their beloved leader to its resting-place. These, in turn, bore the coffin (which was of plain polished oak, enclosing another of lead) on their shoulders. They used neither bier nor pall, but, with rigid simplicity, laid the remains of their honoured friend in the grave. The vast concourse evinced, by their tears and reverent silence, the depth of their emotion. Yet the well-grounded faith of the departed's endless participation in celestial joys predominated over the sense of their own present loss.

The place of his interment is now surrounded by houses and high walls. It adjoins Coleman Street, Bunhill Row, and is one of the shut-up burial-grounds of London. About the year 1757, during the removal of a wall at this spot, the workmen came upon the coffin of George Fox. On it they found a plate bearing his initials, his age, and

an almost obliterated inscription. Curiosity induced them
to raise a portion of the lead, which then disclosed the
features in good preservation. But soon after the admission of the air, little remained but the hair and skeleton.
The Friends had the coffin resoldered and re-interred, and
placed a small stone with the initials "G. F." in the
adjoining wall to mark the spot.

Notwithstanding his great indebtedness to the theology
and ecclesiastical system of which the General Baptists
had previously been the chief expositors, George Fox
was a man whose own special work was a noble and influential one. He stood out amongst his coadjutors as a
marked superior. Burrough, Audland, Naylor, and Pen-
ington may have equalled him in fervour of spirit, and
surpassed him in eloquence, but they lacked his shrewd
common sense, and remarkable executive capacity. In
these latter gifts Penn may have been comparable to
him, but he again fell far behind in the fire of soul and
the indomitable courage possessed by Fox.

The life of George Fox presents an instructive example
of the gradually developed ripeness of character and increasing freedom from error which accompany prayerful
perseverance in the Christian course. There was " first
the blade; then the ear; then the full corn in the ear."
His prayerful reverence, humility, and disinterested de-
votedness to God's glory were his eminent characteristics.
His holiness of life was intimately associated (as all true
holiness must ever be) with a sense of his entire and
abiding dependence upon the Lord for every good gift and
qualification for service. With him, as with all true
Christians, growth in grace was a growth *downwards*

in childlike dependence upon the Lord. His fruitfulness
in the religious life sprang (as it always must do) from an
increasing conviction of the daily, hourly necessity of
leaning on the Lord alone, and of wholly distrusting one's
self and one's own good resolutions. His experience was
like that of Henry Venn, in after days, who records,
" True holiness is quite of another character, than we, for
a long time, in any degree, conceive. It is not serving
God without defect, but with *deep self-abasement*—with
astonishment at His infinite condescension and love manifested to sinners."

Even on some points of doctrine respecting which
fairness has compelled us to criticise George Fox, it is
right to remember that his one-sidedness, as to certain
truths, sometimes resulted from natural reaction against
opposite errors. He saw that many Christians dwelt
too exclusively on some of the offices of the Lord Jesus
Christ, to the forgetfulness or obscuration of others.
Hence he sought to invite men to honour Christ in other
of His offices, as the Sanctifier and Everlasting Teacher
of His church; and as the Saviour, who has emphatically
laid down holiness and obedience as the indispensable
condition of the final acceptance of His people, and who
has solemnly declared of His Father, " Every branch in
Me that beareth not fruit *He taketh it away;*" and " If
a man abide not in Me, he is cast forth as a branch, and
is *withered*." (John xv.)

But the most strenuous and fervent efforts to compass
all truth will ever fail of complete success on this side of
eternity. Truth is infinitely vast and many-sided. The
noblest, wisest, and best of men, can but obtain a partial

knowledge of her innumerable perfections. Even a Humboldt, a Newton, or a Faraday, could acquire but a knowledge of a portion of the illimitable realms of nature. How much more limited, then, must be the best human conception of the Omnipotent and Eternal God of nature and of the universe of worlds!

Hence the function of sects and of leaders of sects is to maintain a special watchword in respect to certain aspects of the infinite Truth of God, which, amid the vastness and boundless variety of its manifestations, might otherwise be too little heeded by creatures as finite as ourselves. As, in a University, each great branch of knowledge has (and needs to have) its own professor or its special advocate, so, in the Church Universal, each of the more prominent aspects of Christian truth may require distinctive exponents for the well-balanced development of the faith of a united Christendom.

It is but a sentimental, or at best a thoughtless, feeling which leads to such frequently-heard exclamations as, " Oh, what a nice thing it would be if there were no sects amongst Christians, if all the churches were united cordially in one communion, under one outward name, with one doctrine, one ministry, one discipline!" This unity, if it is to imply *uniformity*, would be intolerable and deadening. As well might one exclaim, " What a nice thing it would be if all England were as flat as Lincolnshire, or if every flower in every garden were a white lily, and every tree everywhere an oak, and all the genera and species of plants and animals reduced to one!"

A uniform sameness of opinion in the churches is similarly the wish of an idle dream, and would be incompatible alike with a healthy reciprocal action and reaction, and with an appreciation of the vast riches of Divine truth. Harmonious variety is the everlasting condition of God's fair creation, both spiritual and natural. But harmony is absolutely necessary, and happily it is perfectly compatible with infinite variety. Its essential source is readily recognised by all Christians—in love to the one Divine Father, to His dear Son our Saviour, and to His Holy Spirit, who graciously bestows on man His outwardly-recorded revelation of the Bible, and, in connection with its obedient use, His *inward energies* and sanctifying *individualising* influences. To these latter, in particular, George Fox and the Friends have borne a special testimony, which, both directly and indirectly, has rendered an invaluable service to the universal church.

It should ever be remembered that the unity of the Godhead is compatible with a triune *manifestation*, that there are "seven Spirits before the throne," and that the pure light of truth, like that of the sun and of the celestial rainbow witnessed by the beloved Apostle in his Apocalyptic visions, is also "sevenfold"—that is, varied in its harmonious unity of perfection. And so, likewise, with the light of Divine truth; that truth is varied, yet, if we see it aright, will ever appear harmonious. But, as the earnest-hearted Frederic Robertson has reminded us, the harmony and life of perfect truth are best approximated, not by the isolation of its component parts, neither by a mere middle course, but by the lively *union* of its apparently opposite manifestations, and by our best efforts to hold *all* its constituents in their full breadth and *scriptural symmetry.*

A very essential element of this scriptural symmetry of truth consists in the full practical recognition of the great doctrine which George Fox and the Friends have specially borne testimony to—the individualising and perceptible guidance of the Holy Spirit. There is still an unabated need for the continuance of this Quaker testimony. The too gregarious characteristics of other Christian churches, and the almost universally-diffused habit of devolving increased responsibility upon already overburdened pastors, call for continued zeal in the exhibition of the energising individuality of the system of the Society of Friends.

But that Society may be now in danger of lowering its high and noble standard. There is now a peril before it, of seeking to assimilate its principles too much to those of other sects for the sake of proselytism or church extension. May this hitherto eminently-useful body be preserved from losing its remarkable power by a vain attempt to grasp at numerical extension! Such an attempt *must* be futile; for Quakerism (as all its history and experience prove) *is utterly unfit for the many*. The great mass of mankind *cannot*, and will not, be imbued with it, because it is too restraining and too eclectic for them. Its special function consists in indirectly *influencing* the world for good through the medium of a comparatively few disciplined independent spirits, calling no man master in a religious sense, seeking the glory of God and the welfare of their fellow-men, but relying for aid, in each of these two objects, upon the promptings and heaven-given power which the cultivation of prayerful individual responsibility peculiarly cherishes by its more practical realisation of God's own government in the soul.

It would therefore appear that the Friends may with advantage assume that their best interests and most extensive influence in the world will continue to be contingent upon their restricting their Society to those adherents only who can be well and cordially leavened with this distinctive spirit of Quakerism. These will necessarily be but very few, as mankind now are and always have been constituted.

Religious and moral influences are always produced by the concentrated faith and determined effort of individuals, rather than by the mere inertia of homogeneous human masses. For example, the intense will and feeling of such individuals as Wesley, Wilberforce, or Fox, have accomplished mightier good amongst mankind than all the combined influence of the hundred millions of China, Russia, and Hindostan. Christian power consists in developed quality infinitely more than in numerical quantity.

The system of birthright membership is a strikingly inconsistent anomaly, which has greatly injured the Friends as a body. This might well be modified so far as only to involve the retention of the children of Friends in the Society on their making a solemn and thoroughly cordial choice of its communion, on attaining a certain reasonable age.

Let the disciplinary care of the Society for its members be lovingly but effectually exercised, its thoroughness of educational provision for all its offsprings perseveringly continued; let its sympathy with differing sects be charitably and judiciously exercised, in conjunction with the needful separateness; and, above all, let its members cherish, with the most determined tenacity, their distinctive hereditary privilege of being a theocratic democracy, an equal Christian priesthood; each one zealously cultivating the sacred habits of *individual* access to God through the Holy Spirit, whether in public silent worship, or in the privacy of domestic devotion, or amid the activities of daily life. For it cannot be too often remembered that hereafter "*each* one *must* give an account of *himself* to God," and of his individual influences upon others, irrespective of the authority and current opinions of any human society.

As the Friends adhere to this policy of *individualisation and selection*, their numbers will indeed be few, but, what is of far greater importance, their real influence upon mankind, their power of example, their moulding grasp upon the civil and religious world, may be even more remarkable and more beneficial, than, through the good providence of God, it has continued to be for the past two centuries.

Thus fewer proselytes will be gained, but a higher Christian life will be exhibited to the world, a more pleasant and harmonious denominational action maintained, and the salvation of many more souls promoted, both within this sect and far beyond its borders, to the advantage of the other branches of the one church of the Lord Jesus Christ—that glorious Lord whose boundless love is the great object and source of the Holy Spirit's influence, whether exerted upon congregations or in the hearts of private individuals.

There never was a time when the distinctive Quaker element of religious individualisation more needed recognition than in the present day. For now that the population of the world has become so vast, and that both in social and religious movements men act so increasingly in numbers and in masses, the comforts and responsibilities implied in the truth of the Holy Spirit's individualising influences should specially be borne testimony to.

As the modern Christian moves along amongst the crowds of million-peopled cities, he is peculiarly tempted to exclaim, "Will God, and does He, take cognisance of me who am but a mere unit in all this multitude?" Or as he voyages to India or Australia, and gazes week after week, and month after month, upon the illimitable ocean, again the tempting thought arises, "Am I of any account to the Creator of all this profundity and vastness?" Or when availing himself of other facilities of travel, he visits the Alps, or Himalayas, the Rocky Mountains, or the boundless prairies of the Far West, still that thought accompanies him—"What, then, am I?" And perhaps he feels it more strongly than ever, when, on successive Sabbath afternoons, he pensively paces the avenues of great cemeteries, and, for hours together, meets an endless succession of tombstones, each one of which records, in a line or two, the past existence of a being who filled up twenty, or fifty, or eighty years of thousandfold incident, joy and sorrow, and then passed away, leaving but a little dust as his representative on earth, and an obscure epitaph as his memorial; then, again, as the thoughtful visitor looks upward to the infinite expanse of heaven beyond which he knows yet further, that countless worlds like his own, extend in a universe of overpoweringly awful sublimity, then with almost crushing force comes the insinuating fear, "Surely *my* way is hid from the Lord, and *my* judgment passed over from my God, surely I am

but as the minute ephemeral insect which enjoys the sunshine of one summer day, and on the morrow is utterly
lost to observation and existence."

And it is not sufficient to attempt to counteract such
saddening thoughts with anything but the *whole* remedy
of the revealed Christian system. It is not merely enough
to plead in reply that God's unlimited power of regard for
the smallest of His creatures is visibly shown in the
infinity of minute but glorious beauty revealed by the
microscope in flower and insect. Nor is it even sufficient
to remind the humiliated person that Christ died for
him, and that he possesses the Bible and an outward
church.

For he may instantly reply (or, at least keenly feel, if
he does not venture to reply)—"The Lord Jesus lived
and died far away and eighteen hundred years ago, but
what have you or others ever seen or known of Him, now,
personally, positively, *perceptibly?* Where *now* and for
myself is the hope of His coming, and where *now* the
promise of His appearing? And as to the Bible, to say
nothing of the various interpretations of it by each
Christian church and sect, how often have I perused its
pages with a yearning desire to derive from it a sure and
certain hope, a vigorous and vivifying confidence—and
how often have I felt meanwhile as dead and spiritless as
though I mused upon the mystic hieroglyphics of Assyrian
or Egyptian sculpture! My inmost soul craves for some
real power, some piercing light, some enthusiastic energy,
some firm ground of confidence, even additional to that
which you have kindly indicated. Has the Lord Jesus,
has the Bible, given us a hope of such completing and

indispensable blessing? Can you tell me of a source of confidence which shall realise the apostolic definition that 'faith is the *substance* (or anticipative verification) of things hoped for, the *evidence* (even here below, strong and soul-satisfying) of things not seen as yet.' How shall I truly ascertain the actuality of God's Fatherly care for my weak, poor, and insignificant personality, amongst the overpoweringly vast infinities of His creation?"

It is to this craving hunger of the soul, this peculiarly discouraging, but too common insinuation of unbelief, that the individualising system of the Society of Friends specially affords a consoling answer.

For it says, in effect—Let every one who reads in his Bible of the love of the Lord Jesus, of the great sacrifice of His thirty-three years' Incarnation, and of His death on the cross, of His resurrection and ascension and promised future reappearing, let every such one also seek to realise *in himself* the actuality of the glorious promise of the Holy Ghost, in speaking of whom our Lord said: "It is *expedient* for you that I go away. For if I go not away the Comforter will not come unto you; but if I go away, I will send Him unto you." For our Lord also admitted that neither the Scriptures nor the outward preaching of the Gospel were alone sufficient to bring home to the heart with strong faith the testimony of Jesus—inasmuch as He declared, "*He* shall receive of Mine, and shall show it unto you;" and again, "*He* shall testify of Me."

And this truth abides the same. Still our corrective of heart-thirst, our deepest evidence of faith, our satisfying proofs of the individualising love of our

Heavenly Father, must have their source mainly in the felt, *perceptible*, manifestations of Divine love and energy to each.

But the Bible is the essential *test* and indispensable auxiliary of such inward proofs and energies. As we are animated by its glorious revelations of Christ's love, of immortal joy in Him, of the duties of obedience and the appointed path of discipleship; as we accompany these with persevering prayer, as a *procuring* and *intensifying* means—then we receive, *in addition*, perceptions, energies, confidences, joys, pointings of duty, assurances of gracious Divine regard, which, although inward, and incommunicable to other persons, are yet as satisfactory and sure as our universal consciousness that we exist and exercise our senses on outward objects.

When the strength of this certainty becomes dim, it must be renewed and maintained by increased heed to the Holy Scriptures, by more fervent prayer, by more faithful obedience : and then again the Holy Light, the Divine sunshine, brightens afresh upon the soul.

And so, as life and experience proceed, we are enabled more and more clearly to trace indications of God's spiritual interposition in our behalf. Further, we often see it accompanied by manifest concurrences of outward providence attendant on our path. We perceive that in prayers answered or withheld, in blessings bestowed, in trials permitted, in impressions received, in the indications of the applicability of *general* scripture precepts to our own *present and individual circumstances*, and above all in the heart-inspiring assurances of a joyful immortality, through the love of Him who declared "The dead *are* raised," and " I am the Resurrection and the Life "—in all these experiences we may each realise, more and more, as life continues, the preciousness, and the attainable actuality, of that pre-eminent blessing—the *individualising* presence of the Holy Spirit of God and of His dear Son our Lord and Saviour Jesus Christ.

THE END.

R. BARRETT & SONS, Printers, 13, Mark Lane, London.

Printed in the United States
129720LV00006B/141/A

9 781432 642395